ENGLAND OUR ENGLAND

Books by Vernon Coleman

The Medicine Men (1975)
Paper Doctors (1976)
Everything You Want To Know About Ageing (1976)
Stress Control (1978)
The Home Pharmacy (1980)
Aspirin or Ambulance (1980)
Face Values (1981)
Guilt (1982)
The Good Medicine Guide (1982)
Stress And Your Stomach (1983)
Bodypower (1983)
An A to Z Of Women's Problems (1984)
Bodysense (1984)
Taking Care Of Your Skin (1984)
A Guide to Child Health (1984)
Life Without Tranquillisers (1985)
Diabetes (1985)
Arthritis (1985)
Eczema and Dermatitis (1985)
The Story Of Medicine (1985, 1998)
Natural Pain Control (1986)
Mindpower (1986)
Addicts and Addictions (1986)
Dr Vernon Coleman's Guide To Alternative Medicine (1988)
Stress Management Techniques (1988)
Overcoming Stress (1988)
Know Yourself (1988)
The Health Scandal (1988)
The 20 Minute Health Check (1989)
Sex For Everyone (1989)
Mind Over Body (1989)
Eat Green Lose Weight (1990)
Why Animal Experiments Must Stop (1991)
The Drugs Myth (1992)
How To Overcome Toxic Stress (1990)
Why Doctors Do More Harm Than Good (1993)
Stress and Relaxation (1993)

Complete Guide To Sex (1993)
How to Conquer Backache (1993)
How to Conquer Arthritis (1993)
Betrayal of Trust (1994)
Know Your Drugs (1994, 1997)
Food for Thought (1994, 2000)
The Traditional Home Doctor (1994)
I Hope Your Penis Shrivels Up (1994)
People Watching (1995)
Relief from IBS (1995)
The Parent's Handbook (1995)
Oral Sex: Bad Taste And Hard To Swallow? (1995)
Why Is Pubic Hair Curly? (1995)
Men in Dresses (1996)
Power over Cancer (1996)
Crossdressing (1996)
How To Conquer Arthritis (1996)
High Blood Pressure (1996)
How To Stop Your Doctor Killing You (1996)
Fighting For Animals (1996)
Alice and Other Friends (1996)
Spiritpower (1997)
Other People's Problems (1998)
How To Publish Your Own Book (1999)
How To Relax and Overcome Stress (1999)
Animal Rights – Human Wrongs (1999)
Superbody (1999)
The 101 Sexiest, Craziest, Most Outrageous Agony Column
    Questions (and Answers) of All Time (1999)
Strange But True (2000)
Daily Inspirations (2000)
Stomach Problems: Relief At Last (2001)
How To Overcome Guilt (2001)
How To Live Longer (2001)
Sex (2001)
How To Make Money While Watching TV (2001)
We Love Cats (2002)

novels
The Village Cricket Tour (1990)
The Bilbury Chronicles (1992)
Bilbury Grange (1993)
Mrs Caldicot's Cabbage War (1993)
Bilbury Revels (1994)
Deadline (1994)
The Man Who Inherited a Golf Course (1995)
Bilbury Country (1996)
Second Innings (1999)
Around the Wicket (2000)
It's Never Too Late (2001)
Paris in My Springtime (2002)

short stories
Bilbury Pie (1995)

on cricket
Thomas Winsden's Cricketing Almanack (1983)
Diary Of A Cricket Lover (1984)

as Edward Vernon
Practice Makes Perfect (1977)
Practise What You Preach (1978)
Getting Into Practice (1979)
Aphrodisiacs – An Owner's Manual (1983)
The Complete Guide To Life (1984)

as Marc Charbonnier
Tunnel (novel 1980)

with Alice
Alice's Diary (1989)
Alice's Adventures (1992)

with Dr Alan C Turin
No More Headaches (1981)

ENGLAND OUR ENGLAND

A Nation in Jeopardy

Sound Reasons To Reject The
Euro And The EU

Vernon Coleman

BLUE BOOKS

Published by Blue Books, Publishing House, Trinity Place, Barnstaple, Devon EX32 9HJ, England.

Reprinted 2003 (twice), 2004 (twice)

ISBN: 1 899726 21 7

A catalogue record for this book is available from the British Library.

Printed by J.W. Arrowsmith Limited, Bristol

Dedication

This book is all about freedom and individuality.

England Our England is dedicated to the memory of Winston Churchill, William Shakespeare and the other great Englishmen and Englishwomen who must now be spinning in their graves as the country they loved, respected, fought for (and in so many cases died for) is torn apart and threatened with extinction.

It is dedicated to my parents, who fought in a war to protect my English way of life; and to their friends and colleagues who died defending the same constant dream.

It is also dedicated to all other Europeans, whose individuality and national qualities should be cherished and nurtured, not suppressed and hidden away within the monstrous regimentation of an EU superstate. Vive les differences! How dull life would be without them.

And it is dedicated, of course, to Donna Antoinette, my beloved Welsh Princess. Dedicating a book defending England to a Welsh Princess helps define the difference between proud but innocent patriotism and crude, arrogant racism.

Preface

The European Union is widely regarded as a rather annoying joke.

When people think of the EU they tend to think of butter mountains, wine lakes and daft rules about straight bananas. We smile at the knowledge that the EU directive on the export of duck eggs runs to an immodest 26,911 words, and that the EU produces new regulations and laws faster than any individual could possibly read them.

There is a nationwide tendency to think that the crooked, laughably incompetent officials in Brussels are somehow irrelevant and insignificant to our daily lives; no more than an expensive, international extension of the civil service.

But the EU is no joke.

If it is, then the joke is on us.

There has been squabbling and fighting in Europe for three millennia. There have been wars, crusades, plague, pillage, partition, duels, vendettas, invasions, regicides and genocide.

Caesar, Charlemagne, Pope Innocent III, Napoleon and Hitler all tried to unite these countries under a single flag. They all failed.

Now pasty-faced, wooden-headed, clog-footed petty bureaucrats think they can drag all these very individual countries together, eradicate national characteristics, and produce an economic unity. For what? Exactly what is the purpose of this bloodless coup?

It is no exaggeration to say that the European Union poses the greatest threat to democracy, and to our freedom and privacy, that there has ever been.

With astonishing nerve, EU proponents claim that the EU stands for liberty and freedom, and that because secession would destroy the EU, secession must be a threat to freedom and liberty. (That false argument isn't original. It was used in far more logical circumstances by Abraham Lincoln in 1861 and I suspect it wasn't original even then.)

The real truth is that fighting the EU is desperately urgent. We don't have much time left. If you are a European, or you live in Europe, fighting against the EU for what remains of our democracy, our independence and our freedom really is the most important war in the world. The war against the EU is far, far more important – and far more urgent – than that politically expedient invention 'the war against terrorism'.

In an attempt to explain the truth – and to warn you of what is happening to your world – I've prepared a summary of some of the things you should know about the European Union; facts which the main political parties certainly won't tell you. Your TV station, radio station and newspaper probably haven't warned you about these things. Maybe they don't want you to know about them. Maybe the journalists working for them are themselves ignorant.

As you read this book remember that this is not a piece of science fiction. These are not bizarre, paranoid fantasies.

This may turn out to be the most frightening book you've ever read.

But everything you are about to read is true.

Vernon Coleman, England 2002

1

Papers recently released from the Public Records Office under the thirty year rule show that England's former Prime Minister Ted Heath was utterly committed to getting England into the EU (then known as the Common Market) and was, it seems, prepared to do virtually anything to make sure that it happened.

Heath was so eager to help 'sell' England into a new European state that he deliberately deceived the electors to hide from them the consequences of his actions.

Heath knew that the Common Market was the beginning of a one nation European superstate – but he told electors that this would not happen.

Heath knew before he entered into negotiations that there were plans for monetary union. He was told by the Treasury that Common Market countries would have to surrender their sovereignty and hand over management of vital issues to a small group of European administrators. English civil servants warned that once started, the process of change would be unstoppable. A secret Foreign Office memo in 1971 described the Common Market as a 'process of fundamental political importance implying progressive development towards a political union.' The public were told none of this.

Heath's Government was desperate to suppress the truth about entry to the Common Market because polls taken at that time showed that a clear majority of voters were against joining and a clear majority wanted a referendum on the subject.

'There is no question of England losing essential national sovereignty' insisted Heath's Government in 1971. 'The English safeguards of habeas corpus and trial by jury will remain intact. So will the principle that a man is innocent until he has been proved guilty.'

Maybe Heath and his political pals had their fingers crossed when they said this. Maybe they really were more naive than now seems possible.

In 1973, when he wanted to persuade the English people that joining Europe was a 'good thing', Heath promised Parliament that we were only joining a 'trading partnership'.

Two decades later he admitted that he had known all along that England was signing up to a Federal Europe. It seems to me difficult to understand why that was not treason.

2

During negotiations to join the Common Market, Heath was told that English fishing interests would have to be sacrificed if England was to join the Common Market. The EU said that other countries wanted access to English fishing waters. The other negotiators probably didn't expect Heath to give in to this demand (they would have asked for more than they expected) but Heath (being generous with something which didn't belong to him) surprised them by agreeing to their demands. A civil servant described England's 22,000 fishermen as 'expendable'; a view which seems to have been held by Heath, who presumably regarded such a minority group as politically insignificant.

When England was being considered for entry to the Common Market, the six original members realised that England, together with three other new members (Ireland, Denmark and Norway), would control 90 per cent of Europe's fishing.

The six existing members arbitrarily decided that these profitable fisheries should be a 'common European resource' and effectively confiscated them as part of the price for England's entry.

Heath's Government realised that if the nation knew what the Common Market was demanding there would be an outcry both inside and outside the House of Commons. So they dealt with this political hot potato by claiming that English fishermen and fisheries would be protected.

(Deceit did not start with Blair's Government, though they have taken it to new levels.)

The result has been the virtual destruction of both English fisheries and the English fishing industry.

Throughout the period when England's entry to Europe was

under consideration, Heath's Government successfully 'managed' the news media in England. Talk of federalism was banned and major news outlets deliberately gave coverage only to stories which promoted the idea of the Common Market.

And yet while Heath was insisting that we were joining up solely for better trading opportunities, the Prime Minister of Luxembourg stated that: 'The long term objectives of European Monetary Union are very far reaching indeed ... and the degree of freedom vested in national governments might be less than the autonomy enjoyed by the states of the USA.' (That comment was only released in 2001.)

3

'All our past acclaims our future:
Shakespeare's voice and Nelson's hand,
Milton's faith and Wordsworth's trust in this
Our chosen and chainless land,
Bear us witness: come the world against her,
England shall yet stand.'
ALGERNON CHARLES SWINBURNE

4

By 1975, Ted Heath was out and Harold Wilson was in No 10 Downing Street. But the deceit continued.

A referendum was held, but English voters were misled into thinking they were voting for continued involvement in a harmless little 'Common Market'.

It was, voters were assured, nothing more than a trading agreement. Moreover, the English were assured that we would be able to use our national veto if we disapproved of anything planned by the Common Market.

Less than half of those entitled to vote in the referendum wanted England to remain in the Common Market. That was the only vote the English have ever had about Europe.

Astonishingly, not one citizen of any of the 15 nations in the European Union has ever been asked if they wanted to join the European Union.

15

5

'Politicians are 'full of shit and after power.''
BRENDAN BARNS, TONY BLAIR'S FORMER RESEARCH ASSISTANT.

6

Power has been gradually transferred to the EU. Hardly anyone has noticed.

During the last few years there have been five European treaties. Each treaty has transferred power from elected national governments to the central EU structure in Brussels. Once power is transferred to Brussels it cannot be renegotiated and cannot be returned to individual countries (except by leaving the EU).

Blair and his Government still claim that England will not lose its sovereignty if it abandons its currency and becomes a fully fledged member of euroland. This is about as true as some of Heath's 1971 eurobabble.

England has already lost control of its farming, courts, fishing, legislation and citizenship.

The English have to weigh their fruit and vegetables in kilos because that is what the EU demands. Central and local Government employees are already measuring distances in kilometres rather than miles. (Road signs in kilometres can be spotted all over the country. When anyone complains, a local jobsworth will simply say it is a mistake and remove the offending sign for a while.)

The English Government is no longer allowed to give aid and assistance to its citizens. (As English plane-spotters found out when they were arrested in Greece last year.)

We have lost the right to be considered innocent until proven guilty, and we are losing our right not to be locked up unless we have done something wrong.

We are losing control of our armed forces, our right to set our own taxes, our financial services, our transport system and our system of justice. In fact, it is difficult to think of anything we aren't handing over to the bureaucrats in Brussels.

7

The EU allowed other member countries to overfish England's coastal waters (often using massive trawlers and huge nets) and as a result once common fish such as cod, haddock, sole and whiting are now endangered and officially on 'protection lists'. In an attempt to deal with this problem the EU has decided that England must cut its fishing fleet by nearly a third.

8

Citizens who voted for a Labour candidate at the 2001 elections effectively gave Tony Blair a free hand to sell (or, rather, give away) what is left of English independence.

Since then, Blair has effectively agreed to the concept of a federal Europe, although this is something that has never been debated in public and is certainly not something for which any politician has ever asked or received authority.

Europe is now a haven for bureaucracy and the EU is run as though it were a private club – there are few concessions to democracy, and the bureaucrats are constantly helping themselves to more and more power.

The EU politicians are building a federal prison rather than a federal state – and they are doing it with our money but without our authority or approval.

When Prime Ministers attend EU meetings, little is known beforehand about what will be discussed. Afterwards, when the deals have been done, it is impossible to undo them.

Enormous changes have been made to England in recent years and yet none of these changes have been discussed in public, debated in the Houses of Parliament or voted on by the electors.

If Blair gets his way we will lose our currency, our right to set our own interest rates, our right to a democratically elected government, our identity as an independent nation and finally, and perhaps most important of all, our right to free speech.

9

'We have tried to impose many things from above. Nothing ever comes of this. We must involve people in the process of government and the people will at once put everyone in their right place.'
MIKHAIL GORBACHEV

10

The European Union is (technically at least) run by the European Council – a committee of Government heads from each of the EU member nations. These politicians meet a couple of times a year, and the purpose of their meetings is to establish policy guidelines for European integration. Member states are obliged to take into account the objectives and the needs of the European Union and the Council is a de facto institution representing and running the European Union.

When Tony Blair attends the European Council he does not do so primarily to represent or defend English interests but to help plan strategy for the European Union.

The much publicised national veto (once described as a safe-guard against a European political state) has, in practice, pretty much disappeared.

Next in the European hierarchy comes the European Commission and its enormously powerful President.

The current President of the EC is Romano Prodi. Mr Prodi was not elected by the public. Indeed, just how and by whom he was appointed seems to me to be something of a mystery.

Since the unelected Mr Prodi attends the European Council (of Government ministers), and the European Commission works under his guidelines, he clearly has an enormous amount of influence and authority.

Mr Prodi has stated that he wants more power for Brussels, that he wants the national veto to be abandoned, that he wants a European army and that he wants individual nations to hand responsibility to Brussels for foreign policy and defence. This either has already happened, or is happening. Under Prodi's leadership the EU is becoming a new European state.

(It was to Prodi, many English readers will remember, that, in an unguarded moment caught by TV cameras, Tony Blair first gave details of his plans for the last election.)

Prodi and the European Commission have enormous power over your life and your family's life. You have no democratic power over Mr Prodi and the EC.

You do, however, have a limited amount of power over the European Parliament. You can vote for a representative – an MEP.

But I'm afraid that to be honest this doesn't mean very much. The European Parliament has very limited powers and authority. The European Council is not legally obliged to take account of any opinions or amendments which come from the EU Parliament.

And just in case any MEP gets too excited, there is a limit on the amount of time for which he or she can address the European Parliament in any one debate. Just ninety seconds. It is nigh on impossible to put forward any cogent argument in ninety seconds.

There is no opposition in the European government structure and most decisions are made in private and in secret.

11

You might imagine that membership of the EU would be of huge financial benefit to England.

But, in fact, England currently pays £1,250,000 per hour as a membership fee of the EU.

This means that you and I each pay around £450 a year for membership of the EU.

I'm not getting my money's worth. Are you?

Not unless you are an MEP.

England receives some money from the EU, but every pound received by England costs the English taxpayer £4.15. (And the money received by England must be spent in ways dictated by the EU.)

In England, taxes have been rising throughout the New Labour years. And yet services have been deteriorating. The explanation is simple: the money that hasn't been wasted on Domes and wallpaper has been fed to the EU monster.

12

*'For God's sake, madam, don't say that in England for if
you do, they will surely tax it.'*
JONATHAN SWIFT

13

The next step for England will be to abandon the pound sterling and to adopt the euro as the sole currency.

The EU and the Labour Government will undoubtedly do its best to hide the truth about the significance of this.

The President of the European Central Bank has, quite bizarrely, described the euro as an 'expression of freedom and democracy'. Just how he would defend this claim I do not know.

It's like describing Cherie Blair as an ordinary English housewife.

The fact is that the people running the euro were never elected. They have no duty or responsibilities to any electorate or, indeed, to any country.

Under a democratic system one might imagine that the electorate would have a chance to voice their feelings if they felt that their economy was not being well run.

But in the EU, the electorate has no voice about such matters. If people lose their jobs, their homes and their savings they have no one to blame, no one to turn to and, naturally, no one to vote against.

No one seems to know who has authority over the European Central Bank. No democratically elected political leader can affect the decisions or composition of the European Central Bank.

Here we are getting so far into Orwell territory that it's easy to lose your bearings and easy to forget that this is for real. (Curiously, and irrelevantly, Orwell's real surname was Blair.)

The presidency of the European Central Bank is currently held by a Dutchman. The French want a Frenchman to have it and claim that a deal was struck for this to happen in a private, late night conversation four years ago. Democracy? Ha.

Argue that the euro and its undemocratic controllers have already disenfranchised millions of new Europeans, and the pro-Europeans will argue that all this is a good reason why we need a single European Government.

And that, in truth, is what the euro is all about.

Let's get this straight: the euro has nothing whatsoever to do with making lives easier for tourists (though that is what euro-lovers use as their main selling point for this *nouveau* currency).

The euro is all about dragging individual nations into a eurostate with no opposition, no freedom and no democracy. To claim that the euro is an 'expression of freedom and democracy' is to spin the truth so thin that it disappears from sight. In 2002, the euro was accurately described as the 'currency of occupation'.

Enthusiasts for the euro will, it seems, do just about anything to get us to play ball.

Writing in the *Financial Times* recently, a high-ranking Labour Party spokesman claimed that: 'Once it sinks in that any English version of the coins will retain the Queen's head, just as other nationalities retain the symbols of their sovereignty, public hostility will begin to subside.'

Patronising? Moi?

Whether our currency bears the Queen's likeness or not is neither here nor there. (As a practical point it is relevant that the EU has said that it won't accept the Queen's head on English euro coins.) I don't think it matters a jot whether our coins and notes carry the monarch's likeness or a picture of a television soap star. That's all irrelevant froth, and the Labour Party's argument is as superficial as the old one claiming that the big advantage of joining the euro is that holidaymakers will be able to travel around Europe without having to buy different currencies.

(If you confront this argument head on it becomes clear that unless you regularly change many thousands of pounds into foreign currency the submersion of the pound into the euro will be of no practical value to you.)

The significance is not the superficial appearance of the coinage but the political and economic consequences of abandoning a traditional currency and adopting a currency which also has to satisfy the very different needs of over a dozen other countries.

If England loses its currency it will have abandoned a sovereignty which has been protected for centuries, and it will have endangered its future economic stability.

If England joins the euro there will be no going back, and

English interest rates will have to match those current throughout euroland – whether they suit our economy or not.

Politicians throughout Europe have long recognised and openly admitted that joining the euro is a political decision rather than an economic one.

The euro is designed to help turn Europe into a single state. The EU President and commissioners cannot claim to run a unified superstate while individual countries retain their own currency. The EU needs England to abandon sterling.

New Labour europhiles are quite desperate to deceive the electorate over this.

When the time comes for the much promoted referendum on the euro, Blair *et al* will insist that the euro is a strong currency.

They will, of course, be telling porkies.

The euro's history does not support that claim.

Indeed, there are a number of observers who believe that the euro is doomed.

Within three years or so, the EU will be enlarged by the addition of a number of poor Eastern and Central European countries. These countries will make huge demands on the EU. The stronger countries will have to pay to support them.

A dozen years ago, when Germany had to support the newly freed East Germany, the burden was acceptable because Germans were delighted to have a united country again.

Will the previously prosperous citizens of Europe really be happy to see their currency and standard of living debased by a union with these poorer countries? Will the French be happy to see the euro sink so that Poland can be incorporated into the EU?

I think not.

The future for the euro could be far bleaker than Blair dares to admit.

It is worth remembering that when John Major took England into the Exchange Rate Mechanism (ERM) in 1990, the results were disastrous. The pound was locked into a fixed exchange rate with European countries for less than two years but during that time English business had its worst recession for sixty years.

Unemployment doubled, and there were more bankruptcies than in any previous two year period. England lost £68 billion and 100,000 businesses went bust as a direct result of our membership of the ERM. A million people lost their jobs. To avoid total collapse, England had to leave the ERM. (Major and Lamont, the architects of this disaster have a clutch of lucrative appointments and are both doing very nicely now, thank you. However, I suppose we do owe them one small thanks. If England had remained in the ERM we would have probably joined the euro by now.)

But English politicians in all parties are determined to push England into the euro. If we do join, England will hand over control of its economy to Brussels. The greater part of our gold and dollar reserves must be given up and handed over to the European Central Bank.

Whoa!

Read that bit again.

We just hand over our gold and dollar reserves to some people we don't know?

Englishmen and Englishwomen have fought for centuries to protect their country's freedom. Have our leaders forgotten that financial independence is essential for freedom?

The referendum itself is doomed to be something of a sick joke. It is widely assumed that the question the Government will set will be slightly bent (something along the lines of 'Would you like to join the euro and be rich beyond your wildest dreams or would you prefer to sink into poverty?') but what seems certain is that the exchange rate at which we would join the euro will not be mentioned in the referendum.

Blair *et al* will avoid this issue because, although the exchange rate is crucially important, it is something they cannot possibly sort out beforehand.

If England joins the euro (as, I regret to say, looks exceedingly likely, unless you and I work hard to make sure it doesn't happen), the rate at which the pound is locked against the euro will be critical.

When the pound sterling entered the Exchange Rate Mechanism in 1990, the Conservative Government locked England in at an unsustainable, and ultimately very expensive, rate. (When politicians start playing around with money stuff they invariably make a mess of it. They really should restrict themselves to kissing babies, having affairs and telling lies. These are the things they are good at.)

Blair *et al* will doubtless argue that once they have been given the green light by the electorate they will make sure that the pound is converted to the euro at an advantageous rate. But if you think about it, you will see that Blair has about as much chance of arranging this as he has of scoring the winning goal in the next World Cup.

It is widely recognised that the pound is absurdly overvalued at the moment, and has been for some years. The over-valuation of the pound is the main reason why English manufacturing industry is in such a terrible state. Exports have fallen because foreigners simply cannot afford to buy English goods. England desperately needs a devaluation of the pound of at least 10 per cent.

But the other members of the EU are hardly likely to agree to such a devaluation. It is, after all, in their own best interests to ensure that England joins the euro with the pound at a high rate. Does anyone really think that the Germans and the French will give anything away when it comes to negotiating a deal?

The negotiators from the EU know very well that Blair will have backed himself into a very poor negotiating position. Blair will have to agree to whatever rate he is offered by the rest of Europe because he will be stuck between a rock and a hard place.

Is he really likely to walk out of a meeting in Brussels or Frankfurt and come back to England saying: 'I'm going to ignore the referendum; I'm not taking England into the euro because I can't get a decent rate of exchange'?

Of course he won't.

Our quarter-witted Prime Minister (who, I fear, thinks he is cleverer than he is) will have to give in and accept whatever rate he is offered. The Germans and the French will be holding all the cards. England will go into the euro at a rate which will ensure that the nation will be permanently impoverished.

Of course, there is another scenario that could complicate things even more.

If speculators assume (possibly wrongly) that the pound will have to be devalued before England joins, the foreign exchange markets may push the pound downwards when a referendum is called.

This will cause chaos.

As the pound falls, so inflation in England will rise. And when that happens, the Bank of England (now freed of Government control) will have to push up interest rates to make sure that it keeps inflation below the 2.5 per cent target which was set by the Government.

This would have two effects.

First, it would widen the difference between interest rates in England and interest rates in the EU – making entry to the euro ever more painful.

And second, rising interest rates would attract money into England and that would push up the value of the English pound again – thereby making it ever more difficult for Blair to negotiate a decent entry rate.

The chances of Blair and his incompetent ministers dealing with all these complications successfully is surely low. Ministers such as John Prescott and Jack Straw have key roles in the administration of Labour policy. Would you trust these two men (and the rest of the New Labour cabinet) with your financial future?

14

'I have never understood why public opinion about European ideas should be taken into account.'
RAYMOND BARRE, FORMER FRENCH PRIME MINISTER

15

The actual cost of making the conversion from sterling to euro will be great. No, forget 'great'. It will be massive.

It has been estimated that joining the euro could cost England £100 billion. That's a huge chunk of the nation's annual income. Another estimate is that the cost to each individual in England will be in the order of £650. That's a huge chunk out of every annual pay packet.

(A reminder: those who think that permanently exchanging the pound sterling for the euro will mean that they will save money because they won't have to buy foreign currency when travelling abroad should work out what they spend on changing currency each year. I doubt if many people spend more than a tiny fraction of £650.)

On orders from Blair, hospital trusts and local councils are already spending millions of pounds preparing for the euro. (In the case of hospitals, this money is diverted from patient care. It isn't difficult to see where Blair's priorities lie.)

Once England joins the euro there will be no going back. England will be part of a new nation. And England will be governed by unelected administrators in Brussels. Two world wars will have been a complete waste of life. We might just as well have handed over the keys of the Bank of England to Hitler in 1939.

I have no doubt that the English Government will do everything it can to ensure that the English people approve of the euro.

There will, for example, be the threat that if England does not join the euro then decisions will be made by other countries which will have an impact on England but over which England will have no control.

That sounds to me rather like blackmail – and a very good reason for leaving the EU immediately.

Sadly, many members of the public will accept the spurious arguments put forward by Blair and Co.

16

A Dozen Great English Poets

William Blake
John Milton
John Keats
John Dryden
Lord Byron
Thomas Gray
Rupert Brooke
Robert Browning
John Donne
William Wordsworth
Robert Bridges
Geoffrey Chaucer

17

Is it paranoid or rational to wonder if the decision to give the job of manager of the England football club to a Swede could possibly have been influenced by any pro-European thinking? A few years ago, England fans would have been aghast at the idea of their team being managed by a foreigner. The political and media enthusiasm for this appointment has helped encourage the feeling that we are, after all, all Europeans. If the manager of the England team can be born in Sweden, what is to stop the team including players born in Spain, Germany or Italy? The logical next step is to abandon the idea of 'national' sides and to replace that old-fashioned jingoistic concept with 'regional' sides and, possibly, a 'European' side.

18

When the whole of the European Commission was recently found to have been involved in fraud, no one could be prosecuted. Why? Simple. All officials working for the EU have lifetime immunity to prosecution. It doesn't matter what they do. They are untouchable. Moreover, no buildings occupied by EU officials can be searched. And archives are inviolable.

Fraud is endemic within the EU. But there is nothing that anyone can do about it.

For example, in February 1999, Mediterranean shipowners were paid around £30 million of our money for the loss of ships that had been sunk for years. No action was taken against the Commissioner who had authorised the payment.

In November 2000, the EU Court of Auditors criticised the European Commission when it found that £100 million of our money set aside for Eastern Europe and the Balkans had disappeared without explanation. Where did it go? Who has got it? Does anyone care?

In 1999, the EU Court of Auditors claimed that £1.1 billion had been misspent. When they tried to investigate, the Commission explained that documents relating to 2,000 contracts, worth £800 million, had been destroyed. Whoops. It is just so easy to put 2,000 contracts into a shredder by mistake. We all do it all the time. Naturally, no one was arrested.

In 1999, the entire Commission was forced to resign (together with the then President) because of massive corruption within the EU.

However, thanks to the 'immunity from prosecution' rules, no one was prosecuted, and four of the Commissioners who resigned returned to their nice, well-paid jobs. So that was all right then.

Estimates vary, but it seems clear that fraud costs the EU between £4 billion and £8 billion a year.

The annual budget is so badly administered by Brussels that the European Court of Auditors (the official EU auditors) has, for six years running, refused to guarantee the accuracy of the accounts. Imagine the fuss if the auditors for a small company refused to guarantee the accounts? The word 'police' and 'prison' seem to spring to mind.

Waste is endemic in the EU too.

MEPs are forced to claim for first-class tickets and maximum mileage for all their expenses. They are not allowed to claim for what they actually spend, but must claim the maximum or nothing. In the EU the corruption and dishonesty is built into the system. Many of the leading figures in the EU have been (or are currently being) investigated for fraud.

19

'Those who would give up a little freedom for a little security will end up with neither.'
BENJAMIN FRANKLIN

20

EU laws brought in to 'protect' employees mean that someone starting a new job is entitled to take his or her holiday the day he or she starts work.

Thanks to the bureaucrats of Brussels it is, therefore, presumably possible for someone to start a new job, take four weeks' holiday on the day they start, return from holiday, collect four weeks' pay and then leave.

21

The EU is planning to test 30,000 chemicals on animals. The testing programme will involve pointlessly torturing and killing at least 50,000,000 animals. There is ample evidence to prove that the results obtained from this obscene testing programme will be of no value whatsoever.

22

Over the last 250 years, Englishmen and Englishwomen have been responsible for nearly four out of every five major inventions, discoveries and new technologies.

Japanese research shows that more than half of the world's most useful inventions since 1945 were made by Englishmen and Englishwomen.

(Just for comparison, Americans have contributed under one fifth of the world's useful inventions since 1945.)

23

Government is all about coercion – making people do things they do not want to do. In order for Government to work, the people have to know deep down that what the Government is doing makes sense. Otherwise the Government isn't a Government – it is a dictatorship.

24

'All governments ... are against liberty.'
H.L.MENCKEN

25

None of the people in the EU who have the real power, and who take the decisions which control our lives, have been elected. Many have been or are being (or probably will be if there is any justice left in this world) investigated for fraud, deceit, and/or simple crookery.

26

The EU is unconstitutional, flawed and corrupt. It is a fascist state – the opposite of democracy. It is run by selfish, secretive, inward-looking, protectionists who think that democracy means taking money from those who have it, taking a large cut off the top, and then distributing the remains to the have-nots in an entirely arbitrary manner.

27

Under EU law, the Queen of England could be arrested and taken to any other European country for trial. This could be done simply on the basis that a bureaucrat in another European country believed that the Queen had broken (or might have intended to break) a law in that country.

28

'Each country has the government it deserves.'
JOSEPH DE MAISTRE, WRITER

29

Only six per cent of English people think of themselves as European. The figures are similar in Wales, Scotland, Germany, France, Austria and all other European countries. Millions of people want to leave the EU, but they believe the lies they've been told. They fear that outside the EU their country will fail to thrive.

There is no popular support for the EU in *any* European country. The only people really supporting the EU are the bureaucrats who have grabbed power for themselves, and who personally stand to lose so much if the EU is broken up.

30

If we had not been members of the EU, England would by now have accumulated a surplus of cash so substantial that the Government would be able to pay off every householder's mortgage. The future savings would easily be great enough to enable the Government to abolish the tax on petrol.

31

The EU guarantees just two things: more government and more public spending. Neither of these things will be of benefit to the people of England.

32

'The best government is that which governs least.'
JOHN L O'SULLIVAN

33

The English are traditionally rather law abiding. Most of us tend to observe all the rules.

Citizens of other EU countries prefer to play pick 'n' mix with legislation. They are used to bureaucrats being stupid, and they are used to living in countries where there are too many rules, and so they obey the rules which are convenient and ignore the rules which are inconvenient, or which they think are silly.

Too much law produces contempt for the law. (Have you seen the way the French park their cars?)

In England we follow new legislation to the letter of the law. Even if we are ever inclined to rebel, English bureaucrats – who welcome the endless opportunities to be petty-minded which the EU has brought – give us no option.

Other Europeans ignore, or find ways around, legislation which might be a nuisance.

When the EU told the French that they had to start buying English beef again (after the Mad Cow fiasco) the French simply ignored the instruction.

Inevitably, all this puts the English at a terrible disadvantage.

34

'Where all think alike, no one thinks very much.'
WALTER LIPPMANN

35

It is no exaggeration to say that the current chaos on the railways in England was originally created by the EU. The Government had to sell off English Railways because of an EU railways directive. Now the EU wants to put VAT on public transport. And bureaucrats in Brussels plan to take charge of our public transport. They want to coordinate public transport throughout Europe.

36

The sole legitimate function of a government (any government) is to protect human rights. That is why governments were first created. And that is why they exist. There is no other reason. But how many of the things the EU does are done to protect your right to life, liberty and the pursuit of happiness?

It is the duty of those in government to behave responsibly and in the public interest. That is their primary responsibility.

But most of those who have power in the EU are too conceited, too arrogant, too concerned with their own personal futures to put the public interest anywhere near the top of their personal agenda.

37

'It is a mighty fine thing to fight for one's freedom; it is another sight finer to fight for another man's.'
MARK TWAIN

38

The European Parliament has passed a 'Directive on Dietary Supplements' which will ban the over-the-counter sale of effective vitamin therapies and other natural remedies within the EU.

This new ruling was a cause for considerable celebration for the international pharmaceutical industry. For patients and for freedom it was a terrible blow. (Products already on the market can continue to be sold for just three years.)

This is yet another vital reason why England should campaign to leave the EU. Saying 'No' to the Euro just isn't enough.

39

Because the EU now takes priority over the Queen of England, our Government is rewriting the oaths of allegiance.

Policemen, members of the armed forces and civil servants will soon swear an oath of allegiance to the EU.

These changes are already being introduced.

40

The EU wants to ban political parties and all political dissent of which it disapproves. You will not be surprised to hear that the EU does not approve of anyone opposing the EU.

The EU is planning to give itself the power to impose direct rule from Brussels if a member state misbehaves and doesn't fall in line with EU regulations.

The plan (and it will be in force before long) is for the Commission President to be given the authority to rule the countries in the EU absolutely and without question.

You may feel that when this happens we will all be living in a dictatorship.

But by the time it happens (and that will be soon) you will not have the freedom to say so.

41

'Search all of your parks in all of your cities and you
will not find a statue of a committee.'
DAVID OGILVY

42

It seems to be impossible to sack the EU Commissioners.

The Commissioners – who now have more control over our lives than our own Parliament – were pushed off into a very luxurious sunset in early 1999 after the EU was accused of being systematically corrupt and so riddled with fraud that it was widely regarded as nigh on impossible to clean up the mess. The disgraced Commissioners, who clearly didn't want to go, remained in office for six months. They kept their fat pensions.

Subsequently, four of the 'guilty' Commissioners were more or less immediately reappointed. One of those reappointed from this disgraced bunch (England nominee Neil Kinnock – the same freckly faced fool who was rejected by the English electors as a candidate for Prime Minister) was promoted to vice-president and put in charge of rooting out corruption. Kinnock now has more power than he would have had if he had been elected. (These days, the lines between elected and unelected are blurred. In the EU the unelected have more power than the elected. It is salutary to remember that our two EU Commissioners, Kinnock and Chris Patten, now probably have more power as appointed Commissioners than they would have had if they had been elected to run the country.) You couldn't make it up, could you?

Incidentally, there are two Kinnocks now slurping up the gravy in Brussels. Neil's wife is an MEP.

43

Under the terms of the Treaty of Rome, France and Germany have an exclusive right to meet before each Council of Ministers meeting, in order to decide what will happen at the meeting.

44

'He knows nothing and he thinks he knows everything.
Clearly, that points to a political career.'
GEORGE BERNARD SHAW

45

England's trading position with the rest of Europe is now worse than it was when we first joined the EU.

When England joined the EU we had a positive balance of trade with common market countries.

However, within years of joining, England went into the red, and stayed there.

These days we still have a negative trading balance with EU countries.

(To that negative trading balance must be added the huge payments we make to the EU.)

46

England's New Labour Government tried to abolish trial by jury because that is what they were told to do by the EU. (Naturally, Labour politicians did what they do best and lied about it – claiming that they were getting rid of juries in order to make the legal system faster, more effective and more economical.)

The EU is determined to see the end of it, and so trial by jury will disappear soon. If the Labour Government doesn't make sure that juries disappear, the EU will take over and get rid of them anyway.

47

'He who speaks the truth must have one foot in the stirrup.'
ARMENIAN PROVERB

48

Members of Europol (Europe's official police force) are 'immune from legal process of any kind for acts performed ... in the exercise of their official functions'.

So Europol officers can beat you up, smash your property, steal your money, rape you, stick you in prison or even kill you even when there is no evidence of your having committed any crime.

They can do all this and remain beyond the law.

Europol officers are armed and legally able to enforce EU laws in England.

There's one other thing you should know.

One of Europol's first buildings was once the home of the Nazi Gestapo. Just a coincidence, of course.

49

'England is the mother of parliaments.'
JOHN BRIGHT

50

During the European elections of 1999, a 78-year-old pensioner in Liverpool put up a poster for the United Kingdom Independence Party (which campaigns to leave the EU) and wrote on it 'Free speech for England.' and 'Don't forget the 1945 war.'

He was arrested and charged with racially aggravated criminal damage – an offence which carries a penalty of a possible 14 years imprisonment. Only a public outcry led to his release.

51

The BMW-Rover car factory deal failed because the EU's Competition Commissioner said that the English Government could not do anything to support BMW's investment. Such deals are usually allowed in other EU countries.

The result?

Englishmen and Englishwomen lost their jobs. And workers in other EU countries benefited.

52

'Those who deny freedom to others deserve it not for themselves.'
ABRAHAM LINCOLN

53

Scores of universities in England have professors funded directly by the EU. The professors are hired to teach students the value of integrating England into Europe. The cost of these propaganda educationalists is around £600 million a year. This massive sum is, of course, indirectly paid for by English taxpayers.

54

England, the home of the industrial revolution and so much else, now lies 27th in the world league table of gross domestic product per head; 24th in the world in terms of health and fifth from the bottom (out of 29 countries) for adult literacy. England is, however, top of the world table for crime and violence and has the 'worst transport infrastructure' in the so-called 'civilised' world.

55

In the last 30 years, 100,000 pages of new laws, directives and regulations have been introduced – mostly by German and French bureaucrats – to tell us how to run our lives. The EU's unelected bureaucrats have become legislators, investigators, prosecutors, judges, jury, enforcers and executioners.

56

The leaders of the EU want England's trade, England's fish, England's gold, England's oil and England's savings. And they want England inside the EU. They know that if England was independent it would be a major threat to the economy of the EU.

57

'There ought to be limits to freedom.'
GEORGE W BUSH, US PRESIDENT

58

A Dozen Great English Movie Stars

Cary Grant
Charlie Chaplin
Stan Laurel
Charles Laughton
Bob Hope
Dirk Bogarde

Leslie Howard
Julie Andrews
Ronald Colman
Elizabeth Taylor
Vivien Leigh
Lawrence Olivier

59

According to the law, ignorance of the law is no excuse for breaking it. That used to be sensible and fair. Otherwise, of course, everyone accused would plead ignorance.

But that traditional logic is no longer sound nor fair.

Today, even the lawyers themselves don't know the laws. How can ordinary people be expected to know what is legal and what is illegal?

The EU is bringing in new laws faster than anyone can possibly read them. If you sat down today to try to read every law you are supposed to obey you would never finish. And new EU laws now mean that you are also expected to keep all the laws passed in individual member countries of the EU.

So, in addition to being expected to know the laws of England and the laws of the EU, you are also expected to know the laws of Germany, Greece, France, Italy, Spain etc., etc.

As a result, everyone breaks the law these days. It is unavoidable.

This will lead to contempt for the law and increasing lawlessness. The authorities will respond to the lawlessness by introducing more laws and employing more policemen.

This is lunacy.

I suspect that the legal system imposed upon by the EU is an infringement of our freedom and our human rights. It is inherently unreasonable and unfair.

But EU laws forbid us to complain about it.

The laws even forbid us to discuss it.

60

Membership of the EU means that virtually every new piece of legislation involves confiscating property (usually in the form of money) from people who have worked hard to earn it, or who have been prudent enough to save it, and giving it away or using it to fund or finance the unsuccessful. Within the EU this is our present. If we stay in the EU it will be our future.

61

The EU has decided that fire stations in England should get rid of their firemen's poles (originally devised in England around 200 years ago so that firemen could get to their fire engines more speedily). The EU banned the poles because bureaucrats in Brussels were worried that the firemen might hurt themselves. Concern was also expressed that the poles might pose a hazard to blind and disabled employees.

62

It has been announced that voters in England will be given a chance to decide whether or not they want regional assemblies.

Is this a joke?

The structure for these regional assemblies is already in place. It is called 'subsidiarity' and our political leaders accepted it as part of the Maastricht Treaty. Millions of pounds of our money is being spent on enlarging, sustaining and staffing them. The EU Committee of the Regions has nominated representatives who (theoretically) represent us all. None of us voted for them. Does anyone know who they are? Regional assemblies are an integral and essential part of the EU's plan for the future.

If we, the English people, vote 'No' to the proposal of regional assemblies then the Prime Minister will, I guarantee, give us a chance to vote again for Regional Assemblies. And again. And again. Until we 'get it right'.

Once Regional Assemblies have been officially accepted there will be no need for a House of Commons. And England will disappear without trace. The Regional Assemblies will be part of the new EU. The appointed representatives will be supported by a 100,000-strong army of bureaucrats, administrators, advisors, spin doctors and security guards.

(The voters in those countries haven't spotted it yet but the quasi-

Parliaments in Scotland, Wales and Northern Ireland are nothing more than EU Regional Assemblies.)

63

'Injustice anywhere is a threat to justice everywhere.'
MARTIN LUTHER KING

64

Nationalism is defined in the Oxford English Dictionary as 'patriotic feeling' and a 'policy of national independence'.

Racism, on the other hand, is defined as 'a belief in the superiority of a particular race' and 'hostility or discrimination against members of a different race'.

Nationalism and racism are as different as chalk and cheese.

65

In 1948, after the Second World War, the European Union of Federalists was set up in the belief that 'the creation of a united Europe must be regarded as an essential step towards the creation of a united world'.

66

'I have loved justice and hated iniquity; therefore I die in exile.'
HILDEBRAND, POPE GREGORY VII

67

Gradually, week by week and year by year, our EU-dominated government is intruding more and more into the lives of law-abiding citizens.

For example, it has now been decreed that customs officers and tax officials can demand that a taxpayer proves himself innocent. If the authorities say you are guilty of something then you are –

unless you can prove yourself innocent.

Whatever happened to the principle of 'innocent until proven guilty'?

The EU took it away.

Meanwhile, crime continues to rise unabated and criminals go about their business unchecked.

68

It is traditional in England that no parliament may bind its successor; no parliament may restrict the freedoms of the electorate; all law enforcers are subject to the law and everything said in parliament is recorded and published immediately.

In the EU none of this is true.

69

The introduction of spy-in-the-sky cameras (to spy on motorists) is being done on orders from the EU. The cameras are being introduced as part of the EU transport policy.

70

We're fighting for our freedom and time is running out.

71

'Victory belongs to the most persevering.'
NAPOLEON

72

What a tragedy that England abandoned the Commonwealth.

The Commonwealth, allowing individual countries to remain independent but to benefit from trading with one another, would have been an excellent template for the EU.

Maybe England could apologise, beg forgiveness and re-forge those broken links with the Commonwealth countries.

73

Several generations of European politicians have consistently lied about what membership of the EU really involves.

England Prime Minister Tony Blair and his deceitful chums have (for reasons which have never been satisfactorily explained) so much faith in the 'European project', which they seem to regard as both desirable and inevitable, that they seem willing to do anything to disguise the truth, to allay suspicions and fears and to promote the idea of a united Europe.

European politicians do not consult the public, if they can possibly avoid it. If they have to consult, then they are likely either to ignore public opinion or to keep asking the same question until they get the answer they want. Despite the fact that there is remarkably little support for the EU in Europe, there are virtually no major political parties opposed to it.

74

Incinerator plants are being built in England (despite the risks associated with the fumes they produce) although English people don't want them. They are being introduced in order to comply with EU directives on reducing the availability of landfill sites.

75

Half the managers in England say they would not now start a new business in England because of the extra bureaucracy the EU has added to our lives.

76

'When you're fighting a battle you need the will to do what the other side won't do and the ability to surprise and astonish by doing the unexpected.'
ANONYMOUS

77

Tony Blair's Labour Party promised to cut back on red tape if it got into power. But, contrary to this promise, it has issued regulations faster than any other government in history. Since taking office, Blair and his colleagues have introduced an average of ten new laws, rules and directives every day (including Sundays). Many of these new laws have come straight from Brussels.

78

England has been independent, successful and self-reliant for centuries. England has constantly protected and supported other weaker countries, including Wales and Scotland. As a nation, England stands to gain nothing from being a subsidiary state within the EU; a subsidiary region, with considerably less autonomy than Idaho or Alaska have in the USA.

79

In a real democracy, the judiciary   responsible for enforcing the law – has no legislative or executive powers. The law makers and the executors are separate. In the EU (widely recognised to be an inherently corrupt organisation) the same group of unelected people make and enforce the laws.

80

'He who prides himself on giving what he thinks the public wants is often creating a fictitious demand for lower standards which he himself will then satisfy.'
LORD REITH

81

Much of the new employment generated within the EU in recent years has involved the hiring of more bureaucrats and civil servants. In large areas of the EU more than half of all employees are civil servants – working either for the EU or for nationalised industries. Inefficiency and over-employment is commonplace. For example, the Banque de France employs nearly three times as many people as the Bank of England – although both institutions serve much the same purpose. The apparently unceasing increase in the number of bureaucrats in the EU has two adverse effects on the economy of countries within the EU region.

First, the salaries and pensions of all these civil servants add to the growing tax burden.

Second, all these bureaucrats feel they have to do something to justify their existence. And so they create paperwork. The bureaucratic demands they make on entrepreneurs mean that new businesses have to struggle to survive. The economic future for the EU is bleak indeed. Very few EU politicians have ever had a 'real' job in the 'real' world and so they don't understand how damaging this is. (John Prescott, England's Deputy Premier, is one of the small number of politicians in Europe who has ever had a 'real' job in the world outside politics. Prescott used to work as a ship's steward.)

82

EU regulations force public sector organisations to put contracts out to tender across all 15 member states of the EU. When England's Ministry of Defence obediently placed a £5.5 million textile order for uniforms out for tender, the contract was won by a German company. The English textile industry – in crisis and desperately needing work – couldn't compete with the price offered by the Germans. How did the Germans beat the English with a better price? Simple. The German company used cheap labour in Turkey to fulfil the order.

83

If the EU gets its way England will cease to exist within a few years. England will disappear from maps and history books. The Scots and the Welsh will do nothing to help stop this happening – indeed, the evidence suggests that they will almost certainly do everything within their power to hasten England's disappearance.

Those who doubt this should remember that vast numbers of Scots supported England's opponents (whoever they might have been) during the last football World Cup. The Scots and the Welsh think they are on the route to independence. Sadly, they are wrong. Their nations are also destined to become mere regions in euroland. England has supported both Wales and Scotland for generations but active nationalists, scenting the independence they crave, will happily betray England now. The UK is mortally wounded. New Labour is dominated by Scots who have no interest in seeing England survive – indeed, on the contrary, they realise that its destruction is a necessary prelude to European federalism. The reality is that only the English can save England. When there is a referendum on the euro the English should fight for a separate vote. If Scottish, Welsh and English votes are counted together it is more likely that the pound will disappear.

84

Bureaucrats with criminal histories are now in powerful positions in the EU. They cannot be tried because their EU positions give them immunity.

85

We were conned and led into the EU by cheats, liars and traitors.

'There is no question of any erosion of essential national sovereignty,' said Edward Heath in 1975, when talking about the referendum about the Common Market. In 1998, when he was asked if he had known that going into the Common Market would lead to federalism, he said: 'Of course, I bloody did.' So why isn't he in the Tower?

86

'The worth of a State, in the long run, is the worth of the individuals composing it.'
JOHN STUART MILL

87

New EU rules will allow EU courts and EU policemen to keep a defendant in prison for six months before he or she is brought to court to hear what their offence is supposed to be.

88

The main problem with most modern governments is that they consist largely (sometimes exclusively) of lawyers. The only thing lawyers like Blair understand is the law. They live by it and for it. The more laws they bring in the more work there will be for their chums. England in particular (and Europe in general) now has so many laws that even specialist lawyers get confused. New laws are added to old laws, creating constantly increasing confusion. 'Ignorance of the law' is no excuse for breaking the law – and as a result virtually all of us break at least one law every day. The best solution would be for Parliament to be told it had to get rid of one old and out-of-date law every time it wanted to introduce a new one. That makes sense. They'll never do it.

89

'Democracy and socialism have nothing in common but one word; equality. But notice the difference; while democracy seeks equality in liberty, socialism seeks equality in restraint and servitude.'
ALEXIS DE TOCQUEVILLE

90

England's fridge mountain continues to grow at a rate of 6,500 a day. England discards 2,500,000 unwanted fridges each year.

Thanks to new EU regulations, which came into force on 1st January 2002, and which prevent the crushing and burying of old fridges, fridges are now stockpiled on car parks and in fields everywhere. The universally and predictably incompetent English Government has enthusiastically accepted this new EU regulation but has done absolutely nothing about finding an officially acceptable way of dealing with the unwanted fridges (except to write nine times to the EU asking for advice which is clearly not available). Ministers at the Treasury and the absurdly named Department of Environment, Farming and Rural Affairs are squabbling about who is responsible for finding a solution. Before a solution is found the English countryside will be littered with millions of unwanted fridges – all quietly rotting away and releasing their unwanted gases into the air. The French have a healthy approach to EU rules which do not seem sensible (i.e. most of them). They simply ignore them.

91

As a result of EU politics, and because of the infamous Common Agricultural Policy (designed to provide subsidies for French farmers), the average English family has to pay an extra £1,000 a year on food.

92

Modern democracy involves the have-nots demanding and taking money from the haves – or, rather, electing people who do it for them. The EU is run by selfish, secretive, inward-looking, protectionists.

The EU has stolen England's fishing grounds, ruined England's farming industry, put thousands of English businesses to the wall and stolen much of England's oil and gold reserves.

For the privilege of helping weaker countries in Europe, the English have paid a small fortune in taxes and customs duties.

England has become used to supporting Wales and Scotland.

It is absurd and unfair that it should now be expected to support Germany, Greece, Italy and other weaker European countries.

93

Europol has set up files of people who *might* one day be suspected of doing something against EU law (or thinking of doing something against the law). Europol keeps at least 56 different types of information on every suspect. Information stored includes racial origins, religion and political affiliations. Big Brother is watching you.

94

'We the English seem, as it were, to have conquered and peopled half the world in a fit of absence of mind.'
SIR JOHN ROBERT SEELEY

95

Charlemagne, Charles V, Louis XIV, Napoleon, the Kaiser and Hitler all dreamt of creating something like the EU.

96

'Individual MEPs are not an essential, nor even an important, part (of the EU). We are interchangeable bit-part actors, spear-carriers, participating in a mockery of the parliamentary process. Oratory plays no part. Reason plays no part. Our votes cannot change a directive. We are there merely to furnish an illusion of democracy, providing a veneer to conceal what is a fundamentally undemocratic process. The case may change, but the show always goes on, with the actors collecting their wages at the stage door.'
JEFFREY TITFORD, MEP (QUOTED BY ASHLEY MOTE IN *VIGILANCE*)

97

English parliamentary democracy is based on the idea that representation matters as much as legislation. In English law, the state is the servant of the individual. The EU operates on the basis that the individual is the servant of the state. There are no 'free men' or 'free women' in the EU.

98

Back in Saxon times, the Kings of England paid danegeld to the

Vikings to stop them looting, pillaging and burning. The more they paid the more the Vikings demanded. Does that remind you of anything?

99

'...the great principles of habeus corpus and trial by jury...are the supreme protection invented by the British people for ordinary individuals against the state. The power of the executive to cast a man into prison without formulating any charge known to the law, and particularly to deny him judgement by his peers for an indefinite period, is in the highest degree odious, and is the foundation of all totalitarian governments. Nothing can be more abhorrent to democracy. This is really the test of civilisation.'
WINSTON CHURCHILL, 1943

100

England has over £600 billion invested in pensions – that is more than the rest of the EU put together.

England's unfunded pension liabilities are £4,000 per head but that is nothing compared to the debts per head in other EU countries. If England joins the euro we will have to share every other country's debt and our average debt will rise from £4,000 per head to £30,000 per head.

The truth is that other EU countries know that they cannot cope with their pension liabilities and so they want to share our savings.

The EU pension debts are going to be a common liability – with England expected to share the EU's pension debt of £1,200 billion. Vote to join the euro and you will be handing over a good chunk of your pension – and accepting responsibility for paying pensions to Italians, Greeks and Spanish citizens.

It has been confirmed that if we join the euro, some of our pension funds will be handed over to the EU. Indeed, some local council pension funds have already been put into euros to keep EU bureaucrats happy and to help boost the euro. That alone has cost pensioners many millions.

101

England's oil reserves are worth over £250 billion. But the EU now regards them as a shared resource.

What does England get out of the EU?

Well, England get's to share Germany's enormous debts to Russia. That's nice.

102

'The best thing I know between France and England is – the sea.'
DOUGLAS WILLIAM JERROLD

103

European Commission chiefs want a common EU policy on foreign affairs, defence, law and order and spending. They want (and are well on the way to getting) a unified European taxation system. They already have a European Parliament, a European army, a European flag, an EU court and a single EU police force. The EU has a secret plan to introduce a European navy – which will eventually replace the English navy. Citizens in France, Germany, Italy, Spain and other EU countries already use the euro – a universal European currency.

There is a European 'national' anthem and Englishmen and women now carry European passports. There is a European driving licence, a European legal system and a European central bank.

There are virtually no boundaries between many of the countries within the EU. There will soon be regional assemblies to enforce EU laws. And yet our politicians claim that EU bosses don't want an EU Superstate.

Just how stupid do they think we are?

104

'One Conservative Minister, writing about his first visit to an EU ministerial conference (for the Council of Ministers) remarked that on entering the conference chamber he was given a copy of the final

*communique. When he pointed out that the subjects had not yet been
discussed he was told: 'Oh no, sir, the decisions have already been made.
You are here only to sign the communique.'*
ASHLEY MOTE

105

New EU laws pour into England at such a rate that no one can
examine them.

Astonishingly, 90 per cent of all new legislation in England comes
from the EU.

Each and every year the EU passes 3,000 new laws, directives
and regulations – all of which affect our lives. MEPs play little or
no part in approving this legislation. They are just employed as
actors, to make the whole thing look good. And the English parliament can't possibly expect to keep up with all the new laws. They
just pass on the instructions they get from the EU. Not surprisingly,
no one can keep up all the new laws being thrown at us.

106

We have been conquered very quietly. Who did it? Why?

107

England's new Proceeds of Crime Bill is being rushed through
Parliament as yet another piece of legislation allegedly inspired by
the events in America of September 11th 2001. This new bill forces
banks, financial institutions, solicitors and accountants to report
transactions over a certain size to the Government. When the bill
becomes law it will be retrospective. Blair's Government is the first
in history to belabour its citizens with retrospective legislation. This
puts the onus on bankers, lawyers, etc. to think back over any previous transactions (back to the 19th century I have no doubt) and
to report them if they think it necessary. This means that confidentiality is now a thing of the very distant past. Naturally, the
alleged targets of this legislation will be completely unaffected by
it. Terrorists and criminals know how to launder their money and

do so with impunity. It is innocent taxpayers and their accountants who will be caught up in the collateral damage. I suspect that the Government knows this quite well and that the real aim of this new legislation is merely to harass taxpayers.

108

'Society is produced by our wants and government by our wickedness.'
THOMAS PAINE

109

The Maastricht Treaty means that the EU has claim to England's £32 billion worth of gold and dollar reserves. Chancellor Gordon Brown has been selling England's gold – and buying euros – for years. He claims this was a commercial decision – in which case he should sack his financial advisers. Brown has sold 416 tons of gold – more than half of England's total gold holdings – to help prop up the euro, but during this time the value of gold has gradually increased while the value of the euro has fallen. Are the Government's advisers really this incompetent? Or has the Government been buying euros simply in order to move England's gold across to Frankfurt? That has certainly been the result.

110

The EU's courts now take precedence over English courts. An EU judge ranks higher than an English judge.

111

England used to have an excellent small business sector – the best in Europe. But England's small businesses are being destroyed by the EU. Eight out of ten small English businesses do no business outside England but are still subject to absurd EU laws. Less than a tenth of English companies trade with EU countries but thousands of previously successful small English businesses are being forced into bankruptcy by the bureaucrats of Brussels.

112

Popular Sports Invented By The English

Football (Association) aka soccer
Football (Rugby)
Cricket
Snooker
Skiing
Tobogganing
Sailing
Boxing
Darts
Archery
Motor racing
Billiards
Skittles
Baseball (from rounders)
Table tennis
Squash

113

'If I should die, think only this of me:
That there's some corner of a foreign field
That is forever England.'
RUPERT BROOKE

114

Ever since September 11th 2001 the EU has been making oppressive, new laws faster than even the lawyers can keep up with them. The excuse has, of course, been the war against terrorism.

Governments throughout the EU now have laws enabling them to put people in prison without trial – simply on suspicion of terrorism.

Blair and his Government are planning to make it legal for the police in this country (or anywhere in the world) to have access to medical records. Why? The excuse is that it is essential for the war on terrorism. Why do the police in America need to know the names of every English citizen who has taken an antibiotic in the last twelve months? Could this possibly have anything to do with drug company marketing requirements? Why do the police in Germany need to know the names and addresses of all English folk who suffer from depression? Why, come to that, do English policemen need to know the names of every woman who has had a hysterectomy or the names of every man suffering from impotence or premature ejaculation? Isn't privacy and medical confidentiality part of the freedom we are supposed to be protecting? Why hasn't the medical establishment protested about this? Doesn't anyone care about anything that really matters any more? None of this is paranoia. It is all for real. It's happening.

Just before Christmas 2001, the EU passed a new law which will give each country in Europe the right to arrest a citizen of any other country if he or she is suspected of having broken any law in that country, or indeed, of having offended that country in any way (by, for example, making a xenophobic remark of any kind). Without the need to provide evidence of any kind, the arrested citizen can be transported to the offended foreign country and thrown into jail. It does not matter at all whether the crime of which the individual concerned is a crime at all in his home country. He or she might, therefore, be completely unaware of having broken a law. The number of crimes for which citizens can be 'kidnapped' by foreign police forces is extensive. Whatever happened to democracy, the rule of law, human rights and freedom? Gone. All gone.

Within two years it will be a serious crime to make rude remarks about a country. It will be illegal to write anything critical of a country or a religion. It will be illegal to criticise the activities of another country – however foul those activities may be. For example, from 1st January 2004, it will be illegal to criticise a country for allowing bull-fighting.

This new legislation is backed by laws which make it possible for any offended country within the EU to send police into the offender's home country, arrest him and remove him without having to go through any boring extradition process. The legislation outlawing comment on other countries will mean that much of Shakespeare, most novels written with passion, all war movies and many TV series will all be illegal. I am not exaggerating. This is all for real.

The accused will have no appeal, no opportunity to fight the extradition. The police from country X will simply fly to your country, break down your door in the middle of the night, drag you out of bed, put you on a plane and throw you into jail. You will then be subject to that country's customs and expectations.

European governments will even be empowered to arrest citizens who are wanted for questioning, and extradite them without any sort of court hearing. Citizens will have no legal rights whatsoever.

The country wanting to kidnap a citizen will not have to provide any evidence of any wrong doing. And once removed to the foreign country the citizen could, of course, find himself facing a whole range of different charges. A citizen can now be arrested and kidnapped simply so that he can be questioned. This new law entitles each country to make of it whatever they want. In the words of one commentator it is a Humpty Dumpty law.

As if all this was not bad enough, the English Government wants to pass a new law giving it the authority to pass into English law any new crime legislation that may be agreed in Brussels – without the inconvenience of having to take the proposed legislation through the House of Commons and/or the House of Lords.

115

'The process of monetary union goes hand in hand, must go hand in hand, with political integration and ultimately political union. European Monetary Union is, and always was meant to be, a stepping stone on the way to a united Europe.'
WIM DUISENBERG, PRESIDENT EUROPEAN CENTRAL BANK (ECB)

116

The European Central Bank is already having enormous difficulty in fixing a monetary policy that fits the needs of all 15 existing EU member countries. This task will become impossible when the EU expands to include a number of poorer countries. If England joins the euro we will have to share a 'one-fits-all' economic policy with

Romania, Poland, Greece, Malta, Estonia, Slovenia, Lithuania, Latvia and the Czech Republic.

117

There are over 30 crimes for which European nations will soon be legally entitled to 'kidnap' one another's citizen. These crimes include xenophobia and trafficking in endangered plants.

Fraud is on the list of crimes for which extradition must be granted, but whereas in England a prosecutor intending to show that a fraud has been committed must show that there was some intention to defraud, in other countries in the EU an individual who made a genuine error can be charged with fraud.

A café owner in England who accidentally overcharged a foreign tourist could find himself being frogmarched to the airport to face charges of fraud in a foreign court. An English citizen can be arrested for a crime allegedly committed in England and then taken abroad to face trial – even when the crime which was allegedly committed in England isn't a crime under English law.

118

Tony Blair is the greatest threat to England there has ever been. He will sell England to the EU in order to reserve for himself a place at the EU trough.

119

'A government is not free to do as it pleases.'
JOHN LOCKE

120

The EU plans to redefine terrorism as 'acts which seriously affect the political, economic or social structures of a country or an organisation governed by public international law.'

Read that carefully and you will see the scope this new definition will offer to the police. If we give in to the politicians then those who gave their lives for freedom and democracy in World War I and World War II gave their lives in vain.

Obviously any company or political organisation will fall into the category of an organisation governed by international law.

Under this new definition, anyone leafleting or writing an article criticising a multinational corporation will be a terrorist. Anyone who writes an article opposing genetic engineering will be a terrorist since what he does will seriously affect the economic structure of an organisation governed by public international law. Anyone publicly (or even privately) criticising a political party in power will be a terrorist. If this new legislation becomes law (and it will) it will be illegal to write anything derogatory about vaccines, genetic engineering, meat, the farming industry. It will be illegal for me to give you a list of chemicals which may cause cancer. It will be illegal for me to list the possible side effects which may be associated with a prescription drug.

This new law will be added to the existing laws of libel and to a mass of national and EU laws which exist to protect governments and multinationals. Governments respond to protests by pointing to human rights legislation. But when human rights legislation is seriously inconvenient to a government, or might threaten the economic future of multinational, it is invalidated and put aside.

There is, it seems to me, only one thing left for us to do. If you live in a country in the EU you must campaign hard to leave the EU. We must do this now. It will very soon be illegal to be a Eurosceptic. Our freedom, our liberty is at stake. Campaigning against Europe – and the EU – really is now the only game in town worth playing. Everything else can wait. If we don't win this battle we've lost everything. If we don't campaign now against this increasing oppressive European state then we soon won't be able to campaign against anything.

Our only answer is a very simple one: we must fight tooth and nail, to the very last breath, to destroy the EU. This barbarous organisation adds nothing to our lives. It costs a fortune to run and has produced nothing of value.

Sadly, this is a battle we have to fight without the help of most European politicians – the majority of whom are dedicated to the EU. (And is there not something suspicious about that? Most electors in most European countries are opposed to the EU. Politicians tend to go with the flow – and yet no major political parties campaign against the EU.)

What remains of our freedom is at stake. It may be too late. But fighting the EU is our only chance. This is a battle for freedom: as important a battle as we, or our ancestors, have ever fought.

121

A century or so ago men went into politics when they had made their personal fortunes. They were unbribable because they were rich. They had all the money and power they needed. They wanted recognition, immortality and respect. They also wanted (and today, sadly, this sounds strange) to serve their country.

Today's politicians, the ones who are selling England and our freedom, go into politics because they are ill-suited for anything else. They go into politics because they cannot hold down jobs in the real world. They go into politics to make money. They are easy to bribe. They are always on the lookout for ways in which they can make money after they leave government. Today's professional politicians are brought up in a world where deception is everything and perception is not just more important than reality – it has replaced reality and is, to them, the only thing that matters.

122

'Any fool can make a rule – and every fool will mind it.'
HENRY DAVID THOREAU

123

For years we have been losing more and more of our freedom and our privacy. England already has more CCTV cameras than any other nation on earth. Nothing is confidential. The Government and local authorities in England have spent £1 billion of taxpayers' money on CCTV cameras over the last decade. There are now far more CCTV cameras in England than in any other country on the planet. Lots more are planned. A whole industry has developed around these cameras, and countless thousands of people are employed to watch the 24-hour coverage they provide. Most English people seem unconcerned about this gross invasion of their privacy even though there is absolutely no evidence that these cameras reduce crime, reduce anxiety about crime or help solve crimes. There is evidence proving that better street lighting is four times more effective than CCTV cameras at preventing crime. Despite having more CCTV cameras than any other country in the world, England now has the worst crime rate in the world.

What next? Street microphones? Don't laugh. They've already got microphones on the streets in Redwood City, California USA and in Los Angeles USA. Other American cities are planning to follow suit. The courts now accept that when in public places individuals have no reasonable expectation of privacy. They can, and will, peep inside your bag and your pockets without you being aware of it. Actually, you don't have much privacy in your home either. In parts of the USA they are now using thermal imaging to see into people's homes.

Under Labour, the loss of privacy has intensified. And, with the war on terrorism as an excuse, things are about to get much, much worse. Governments everywhere will be monitoring the movements of terrorists, eavesdropping on their telephone calls and opening their e-mails. To do this they will, of course, have to invade our privacy. Actually they're already doing it.

The Echelon system, governed by five English-speaking nations (England, USA, Australia, Canada and New Zealand), and run by America's National Security Agency, uses satellites to eavesdrop on any electronic communication (such as phone calls, e-mails and faxes).

Echelon works by recognising key words from its dictionary of trigger words and phrases. Use the wrong word – and it's very easy to do so in an entirely innocent conversation – and you're likely to have armed policemen banging on your door at 4.00 a.m.

Of course, none of this is really much good in the war against terrorists since terrorists are pretty careful about how they communicate with one another. But the system is good for keeping an eye on law-abiding citizens.

It is, of course, possible to encrypt your e-mails. It is possible to purchase programmes so good that it would take 4,000 years for every computer in the USA, working together, to crack the codes they create. But there's a snag. Encrypt your e-mails and the authorities will assume you've got something to hide. They might not be able to read your e-mail messages but you will have attracted their attention; they will watch you closely and, if they decide that they want to read your e-mails they'll force you to hand over the key. To teach you a lesson, and use you as a warning to others who might be tempted to try encryption, you could well find yourself getting one of those 4.00 a.m. visits from armed policemen. The bottom line: e-mail encryption is pretty much a waste of time. Don't bother.

Now the Government, inspired and encouraged by the EU, is talking of introducing compulsory identity cards. These will be identical to the ones the Nazis used – but more sophisticated. These won't be just the harmless bits of cardboard with a photograph and a name which most people seem to think they will be. These will include fingerprints and iris scans. The excuse is that these are essential to our nation's security. 'If you've got nothing to hide what does it matter?' say the trusting.

It matters because privacy is an essential part of human dignity. And without dignity there is no freedom.

If we allow the Government to impose ID cards on us we are taking a big step towards a police state and losing our freedom: freedom we treasured so much that we fought two world wars to retain it.

In addition to fingerprinting us all, the government plans to stuff these cards with confidential information. The aim is that these cards will eventually carry every bit of information which concerns you: your employment record, whether you are claiming or entitled to social security benefits, your tax records, your medical records, your pension details. If you have a driving licence, the details will be on the card. The card will be your credit card, your organ donor card, your cashpoint card and your passport. These cards will be fitted with microchip satellite-tracking technology so that the police will know exactly where you are at any given time. Go out of your house without your identity card and you will be arrested. Your identity card will carry information about your personal medical records, your personal financial situation, your debts, your assets, your criminal record, your entitlement to state benefits, your employment history and whether or not you have been vaccinated.

Anyone who campaigns regularly will be exceptionally vulnerable – and liable to harassment and arrest. Corporate lobbyists will find it easy to have campaigners arrested and put out of action.

National Health Service hospitals in England already make decisions about whether or not to save patients according to their age, family status and wealth. (Believe it, it's true.) It will be a lot easier for doctors, nurses and bureaucrats to decide whether or not to let you die if your ID card shows that you are alone in the world, pretty much broke and of no great value to anyone.

ID cards – smart cards – can track where you are, where you've been and what you've been doing. They can allow you access to some places and deny you access to others. Iris scans can detect recent drug use. They can confirm your identity and tell what you've been drinking or smoking from some distance.

Who will have control over the information on these ID cards?

Who will be able to 'read' them?

How easy will they be to forge? (Very, I suspect.)

Does anyone seriously think that ID cards will stop terrorists and suicide bombers?

Will the authorities be able to cancel or change the contents of your card without your knowledge? (Cards of this type can be amended from afar.)

How easy will it be for an unknown bureaucrat to reach out and change your details without your knowledge?

How easy will it be for a crook to help himself to all your money?

What if you lose your ID card?

If you lose a credit card it's no great loss: you can easily get another number.

But if you lose an ID card you can't get a new fingerprint or eye print. Crooks, however, can fake these and use your card.

How long before the authorities decide that it will be much more convenient and safer for us all if they put all this information on a microchip embedded in our hands or forearms? The technology is already available.

Will ID cards or microchips contain satellite positioning and tracking technology? (You bet they will.)

What's the moral difference between having a microchip

embedded under your skin and having a number tattooed on your arm?

There is much irony in all this.

We are told that the war on terrorism is all about freedom.

But how can we be fighting for freedom if they plan to take our freedom away from us anyway?

The day after I first published a warning about ID cards, advising readers not to carry ID cards, the Government responded by announcing that it was no longer going to introduce them. They were, they said, never going to introduce ID cards. It was all a misunderstanding. They hadn't ever thought of it. They wouldn't dream of it.

A week or two later, when they thought no one was looking, they quietly announced that they were considering identity cards after all.

124

The European Commission, under pressure from the USA, is desperate to give the green light to biotech companies, but some European governments (under pressure from justifiably nervous voters) are sticking to their moratorium on new modified crops.

Although they have no evidence to support their claim, EU Commission officials are desperately arguing that genetically modified foods are safe.

But the governments which are refusing to allow genetic engineering to continue are standing firm.

However, the ambitious Prime Minister Blair (keen to keep on the right side of EU bosses) is enthusiastically demanding that biotech companies be allowed to start producing new Frankenstein foods again. The EU Commissioners approve of GM crops (because that suits the American Government which is keen to please the relevant American industry) and Blair follows the EU line.

125

'The process of creating and entrenching highly selective, reshaped or completely fabricated memories of the past is what we call 'indoctrination' or 'propaganda' when it is conducted by official enemies, and 'education', 'moral instruction' or 'character building' when we

do it ourselves. It is a valuable mechanism of control, since it effectively blocks any understanding of what is happening in the world. One crucial goal of successful education is to deflect attention elsewhere ... and away from our own institutions and their systematic functioning and behaviour, the real source of a great deal of the violence and suffering in the world. It is crucially important to prevent understanding and to divert attention from the sources of our own conduct, so that elite groups can act without popular constraints to achieve their goals – which are called 'the national interest'.

NOAM CHOMSKY

126

Most people in England still think in pounds and ounces. When Prime Minister Blair and his wife had a new son (Leo), the baby's birthweight was announced in pounds and ounces.

But selling a pound of apples is now illegal in England. Shopkeepers who dare to sell produce in pounds face a £5,000 fine or 6 months in jail. This is because EU law now takes precedence over an Act of Parliament which says that imperial weights are legal. The curious thing, however, is that everyone in Europe still buys three and a half inch floppy disks.

Outside the EU, most of the rest of the world (including America) is, of course, still non-metric and England had an advantage because of this.

Now, thanks to the EU, that advantage has gone.

Incidentally, the leaflet announcing that metrication had now become compulsory, and that a part of English culture was being destroyed, was published in England in Arabic, Bengali, Hindi, Turkish, Chinese, Welsh, Vietnamese and countless other languages – so as to avoid offending those cultures.

England gave Imperial measures to the rest of the world and the rest of world still uses and enjoys that gift. Thanks to the EU, however, the English will go to prison if they try to use it.

Good laws are introduced to prevent suffering. Who suffers if a greengrocer sells apples by the pound? No one. Only the EU complains.

We now have laws to defend the state from the individual. That is fascism.

Good laws are reasonable, generally supported by the people, necessary and capable of being policed and enforced with an appropriate punishment – which is generally known and accepted.

So, how does the EU justify laws banning Imperial measures?

127

The EU, like Burma, Cuba and North Korea, rules by decree and in secrecy. There are no checks.

It is difficult to find out what is going on until it happens. And we pay through the nose to be members.

128

'The effect of socialist doctrine on Capitalist society is to produce a third thing, different from either of its two begetters – to wit, the Servile State.'
HILAIRE BELLOC

129

As long ago as the mid-1980s, the number of laws created by the EU's bureaucrats in Brussels had exceeded the number of laws passed in England in the first 700 years of a parliamentary democracy.

130

The EU wants to introduce a single, pan-European air traffic control system – with bureaucrats in Brussels creating, but not taking responsibility for, the crashes.

131

Postage rates in England were put up to harmonise with rates in the rest of the EU.

132

'The mass of men lead lives of quiet desperation.'
HENRY DAVID THOREAU

133

The EU has announced that keeping chickens in small cages is cruel and will be banned. The ban will come into operation in 2012. Why the delay? Could it possibly be that existing cages will need to be replaced by then anyway?

134

The EU insists that artists now get 4 per cent of the price every time a work of art is resold. Many living artists oppose this non-sense which was first introduced by Mussolini in 1941 (the Italians simply ignored it then and for years afterwards).

Only the English are taking any notice and paying up. The result is that the English art market (the main one in the world) now seems doomed.

What will the EU think of next? Are car manufacturers going to get a percentage of the price when a second-hand car is sold? Are writers going to be paid an additional royalty when a book-shop sells a second-hand copy of their book?

135

England was the first country in the world to develop a free press. But our free press will soon be nothing more than a piece of history. In the EU, a free press will soon be illegal.

136

Duty-free sales were abolished to make the EU look like one big country.

137

Remember: the citizens of Scotland, Wales and Northern Ireland may think that they have taken a step towards independence. They have not. They are simply regions of the European Union.

Scotland, Northern Ireland and Wales have been devolved to fit into the new plan for the European state (and not because Blair wanted to be generous to those quasi-nations).

There will not be, and cannot be, an English parliament because the EU bureaucrats have already divided England into nine separate regions.

This, remember, isn't a plan for the future. It is already happening. New maps of Europe will show that England has disappeared and been replaced by nine regions. Roads in England are now part of a pan-European road system.

The New Labour government has encouraged devolution. But devolution as described by Blair *et al* isn't what it seems. The devolved regions of England just happen to fit the European map of the regions of the new European Federal State.

England will be split into regions and there will be government offices, regional development agencies (members of which are political appointees – there is no voting) and regional chambers in each region.

These regional organisations (which have already been set up and already exist) will be the regional seats of government, answerable to Brussels.

There is much mystery about exactly what the regional chambers will do – although vast amounts of public money are already being pumped into them for 'running expenses'. For reasons which only the bureaucrats can possibly explain, not all new regions will fit into existing nations. Some regions will cross traditional borders.

For example, parts of the south east region of England (Kent and West Sussex) will be considered to be part of a region called Pas du Nord, centred on Lille in France. And parts of London and the South East will be part of the North German plain.

The idea behind these seemingly illogical plans is, presumably, to break down old ideas of nationalism and to help encourage us all to think of ourselves not as 'English', 'Scottish', 'Welsh', 'French' or 'German' but as 'European'.

138

'Those who give up essential liberty to obtain a little temporary safety deserve neither liberty nor safety.'
BENJAMIN FRANKLIN

139

A vote for the euro is a vote for treason.

140

The development of new English regions, to be controlled and run from Brussels, will lead to the abolition of the Westminster Parliament.

In practice, Tony the First and his other senior ministers seem to have decided that the Westminster Parliament is already irrelevant.

Blair turned up for only seven per cent of votes in the first six months of the current Parliament.

That gives him the worst record of any English MP.

Jack Straw, allegedly Foreign Secretary, managed to attend just 15 per cent of the time and Chancellor Gordon Brown managed an equally derisory 17 per cent of votes.

These MPs were elected to represent their constituents. That is what they are paid for. And the House of Commons is their workplace. How many employers would be happy with an employee who turned up just seven per cent of the time?

141

'I think patriotism is like charity – it begins at home.'
HENRY JAMES

142

New Labour threw hereditary peers out of the House of Lords (because they might have made a fuss about New Labour's pro-EU policies) and replaced them with New Labour chums. Curiously, New Labour had originally planned to abolish the House of Lords completely. Now, what we have is less democratic than what we had.

143

These days, most politicians go into politics not because they want to make the world a better place but because they want the prestige, the power, the money and the kudos. Most modern politicians are as vain and selfish as actors – without having the charisma. Top politicians are selected because they have nice smiles and are photogenic.

144

'The top priority (is) to turn the EU into a single political state.'
JOSHKA FISCHER, GERMAN FOREIGN MINISTER, 1998

145

The European Court of Justice (surely the most inappropriately named organisation in history) regards itself as superior to all other courts – including the European Court of Human Rights. The aim of the ECJ seems to be to protect and strengthen the EU.

146

Politicians regard legislation as the answer to every problem. They never consider other ways of doing things. Modern politicians are political nannies; determined to take control of our lives in every conceivable way. It is the EU way.

The real purpose of government (often forgotten these days), is to maintain law and order, preserve justice and provide an infrastructure which makes life good and helps preserve the freedom of the people.

It is not necessary for a government to be forever doing things, interfering in every aspect of life.

147

A Dozen Great English Saints, Leaders, Thinkers and Philosophers

Thomas à Becket
The Venerable St. Bede
Jeremy Bentham
John Locke
Bertrand Russell
Edmund Burke
Francis Bacon
Florence Nightingale
Robert Baden-Powell
Humphrey Davy
William Booth
William Wilberforce

148

Remember: if England joins the euro we will have to take on part of the EU's £1,200 billion pension debt. Your pension will be in peril.

149

'If you make people think they're thinking, they'll love you;
but if you really make them think, they'll hate you.'
DON MARQUIS

150

Under the new EU regional system, Gibraltar will be Spanish (though for Gibraltarians the good news is that Spain will have disappeared and they will be classified as Europeans rather than as Spanish). The EU has regarded Gibraltar as 'Spanish' since 1966.

The EU has offered Gibraltar a bribe of £35 million to agree to joint English/Spanish ownership. Whoops, sorry, did I say bribe? I meant special development grant.

This is clearly an essential part of the overall EU plan. Gibraltar will have to become a part of one of the new regions carved out of the country formerly known as Spain. It would look silly on the new maps of Europe to show Gibraltar as part of Cornwall.

The very best Gibraltarians can hope for is to be a separate EU region. They will have to fight very hard to get that.

When Foreign Office Minister Jack Straw announced that Britain was prepared to share Gibraltar with Spain and the people of Gibraltar protested at this, a Labour Government Minister tried to reassure them by pointing out that the change would simply mean that they would have to fly a Spanish flag instead of a British flag. The Minister genuinely seemed to think that they would be soothed by this. This says a great deal about Blair's Government, but not a lot for it.

151

The Common Agricultural Policy (CAP) is one of the most expensive and destructive pieces of European lunacy. It is the CAP which creates butter mountains and wine lakes. It is the CAP which forces England to import 20 per cent of its milk from France, while English farmers have to pour milk from English cows down the drain. It is the CAP which pays farmers to do nothing with their land through set-aside payments. The better the land the higher the set-aside payments.

152

Unless we leave the EU now, all the men and women who died in the 20th century's two world wars will have died in vain, and will have been betrayed.

153

Political correctness helps to suppress nationalism and patriotism – and helps the EU to thrive and grow stronger.

154

'When privacy is outlawed only outlaws will have privacy.'
CLAIRE WOLFE

155

Don't be conned into thinking that when your region gets an EU grant you are getting something for nothing.

When an English region applies for a grant, the bureaucrats of the EU decide how much to give and how it is to be spent.

The money is not handed over until the project has been completed. So the region has to borrow the money at commercial rates. When the project is finished, an EU inspector (a bureaucrat from France, Spain, Italy, Greece or some other EU country) has a look at it. If he or she is satisfied, then the EU will hand over the promised grant.

But the money was ours in the first place.

The grant the EU hands out comes from money that the English taxpayer had handed over.

So, people who think they are getting an EU grant are simply getting some of their own money back – with massive deductions for overheads, expenses, kickbacks and bribes.

156

The self-employed, and small business owners, are now obliged by EU law to take four weeks' paid leave every year. There are no exemptions.

I'm a self-employed writer. Legally, I now have no choice in the matter. I am legally bound by EU legislation to give myself four weeks' paid holiday whether I want to or not. Why does the word 'absurd' seem so appropriate?

157

It is not enough simply to ignore the europhiles. They will not go away until and unless we make them go away.

158

According to the treaties we have signed with the EU we have already agreed to the '...legal termination of (our) independence, sovereignty and right to self government for all time.' But it is not (quite) too late to change our minds.

159

'To constitute the millionth part of a legislature, by voting for one or two men once in three or five years, however conscientiously this duty may be performed, can exercise but little active influence upon any man's life and character.'
SAMUEL SMILES

160

The big question, of course, is just whose idea was the EU? Who is the secret power broker behind the changes which are taking place?

The greed and ambition of politicians and bureaucrats keeps the EU alive – and help it keep growing – but I find it impossible to believe that the EU just happened. Who is behind it all? Why?

Inept politicians sniffing out power and money and insignificant bureaucrats with their snouts buried deep in the trough did not devise the EU – they simply came along later and helped to sustain the system.

161

Former Premier Edward Heath has admitted that he hid the truth from the English electorate. Harold Wilson did the same. Thatcher claims she was tricked and has now turned against the EU. (Less than a week after Thatcher had declared her opposition to the EU it was announced that she was effectively retiring from public life. How convenient for the europhiles that such a powerful voice should be 'silenced'.) Major secretly gave away power. Blair has given away rights and freedoms with both hands.

162

'No man hath power over my rights and liberties and I over no man's.'
RICHARD OVERTON (POLITICAL ACTIVIST IN THE TIME OF
OLIVER CROMWELL)

163

The new and wonderful European Court of Justice now has the authority to overturn laws made by the English Parliament and verdicts delivered by English courts.

This is because EU courts and laws now take precedence over English courts and laws.

Did you know that? Or did your MP and MEP forget to tell you?

The abolition of the Imperial system of weights and measures was not drawn to the attention of the English people – but it happened and only came to our attention through the efforts of the 'metric martyrs'.

But metrication is really only a superficial problem.

The fact is that the English Parliament surrendered its sovereignty in 1972.

It used to be a principle of English law that where two laws were incompatible the later one was considered to take precedence. This is no longer true. European laws now takes priority over any English laws.

Articles describing the supremacy, role and power of the English parliament are of historical interest only.

Moreover, the European Commission is now using regulations rather than directives or laws. Directives need to be put into the national laws of each member state. But regulations made in Brussels by unknown bureaucrats take immediate effect. Decisions made by European bureaucrats cannot be overturned or ignored.

Our lives are now ruled by regulations created by the same regiments of incompetent European bureaucrats who gave us butter mountains and wine lakes.

164

Make no mistake about it, the fight against the EU and the euro is the most important fight Englishmen and Englishwomen have ever fought. This is a war we cannot afford to lose. There may not be any bullets fired, but this war is more crucial to England's future than any other war in history.

165

If you want to know more about the EU I thoroughly recommend that you read *Vigilance – A defence of British Liberty* by Ashley Mote published by Tanner Publishing. It's impressive, terrifying, depressing, enraging and comprehensive.

166

'The mass of man serve the state not as men but as machines, with their bodies. They are the standing army and the jailers and the constables. In most cases there is no free exercise whatever of the judgement or of the moral sense; but they put themselves on a level with wood and earth and stones; and wooden men can perhaps be manufactured that will serve the purpose as well. Such command no more respect than men of straw or a lump of dirt.'
HENRY DAVID THOREAU

167

English courts are about to get a new system of justice known as corpus juris.

The lay magistrate system in England is to be abandoned, magistrates' courts will be closed and trial without jury will soon be introduced. These changes are being taken so that England can adopt the European system of justice known as corpus juris.

You knew about this, of course? Your MP told you didn't he? The BBC has carried endless programmes about it. No? Gosh. What a surprise.

Under the old English system of justice there were three crucial cornerstones.

First, we were all presumed innocent until proven guilty. Remember that one? Sweet, wasn't it?

Second, no one could be held in custody for more than three days without being charged. (This was known as habeas corpus.)

The concept of habeas corpus was a cornerstone of English justice. (Note the past tense.) It has been around since Henry III at least. Habeas corpus was older than parliament. We will soon be less free and more exposed to the raw power of a totalitarian state than our ancestors were a thousand years ago. Bad King Tony I has given away rights that English citizens took centuries to accumulate. King John was a kindly and compassionate man compared to Tony Blair.

Third, a person charged with a criminal offence was entitled to a trial by jury.

That will soon change.

Under the EU system, the presumption of innocence does not exist, habeas corpus does not exist and there is no right to a trial by jury.

Bad enough?

You just wait. There is more.

Blair has agreed that Englishmen and Englishwomen can be extradited without English courts being asked to decide whether or not there is any evidence against them, and has agreed that English citizens can be extradited even if they have not broken any English laws.

Blair has agreed that English citizens can be extradited even if they have not committed any crime recognised by English law.

The new EU laws create 32 European supercrimes for which any EU country will be entitled to obtain extradition merely by providing evidence that a warrant has been properly issued. The evidence may be feeble, false, outrageous or trivial but no local English court will be able to interfere.

The arrested citizen will be taken abroad, to a foreign court and tried in a foreign language.

That is what Tony Blair has chosen to do with the power which voters gave him at the last election.

We are told that these new EU warrants are a result of the New

York twin towers tragedy of September 11th 2001 but that is just a little bit of a porky if you don't mind my saying so.

Only one of the 32 supercrimes is linked to terrorism and the EU extradition laws were planned long before September 11th. Most of the new laws are designed to catch and punish ordinary citizens.

For example, the number one new EU supercrime is 'participation in a criminal organisation'. Exactly what does that mean? Business laws differ widely around the world. Who defines 'criminal organisation'? How many political parties or campaigning groups will fall within the definition 'criminal organisation'?

The EU seems to have a particular dislike for citizens who speak out and oppose the federalism of Europe.

We are heading for a single criminal justice system in Europe. It is a criminal justice system which may well be a system, but it seems to me to have remarkably little to do with criminals and almost nothing to do with justice.

168

Europe has a common defence policy. It now has a European army. Naturally, it makes sense for an army to have a country to which it can be loyal. Hence, another argument for a European State.

169

Great English Explorers & Adventurers

Richard Burton (orientalist and explorer)
Captain Robert Falcon Scott (polar explorer)
Ernest Shackleton (polar explorer)
Captain Cook (discoverer of Australia and New Zealand)
Sir Ranulph Twisleton-Wykeham-Fiennes (polar explorer)
John Alcock (first man to fly the Atlantic non-stop)
John Hunt (led first ascent of Everest)
John Hanning Speke (explorer)
Malcolm Campbell (world land and water speed record holder)
Donald Campbell (world land and water speed record holder)
Captain Oates (polar explorer)
Sir Francis Chichester (yachtsman)

Sir Francis Drake (navigator and pirate)
Sir Walter Raleigh (navigator and poet)

170

The new EU has the power to adopt laws to combat racism and xenophobia. Sounds fair enough. Sadly, however neither term has been defined.

And that is worrying.

But it is nowhere near as worrying as the fact that the European Court of Justice has ruled that the EU can lawfully suppress political criticism of its institutions and leading figures.

Whoa! What? Can't possibly be true.

It is.

The EU has given itself the power to restrict dissent and to punish individuals who have 'damaged the institution's image and reputation'.

To do this it is using a legal phrasing ('protection of the rights of others') which was used by fascist governments in the 1920s and 1930s.

This extraordinary decision goes directly against the non EU Court of Human Rights at Strasbourg – indeed it defies half a century of case law from the Strasbourg court.

Unbelievably, the EU court has also resurrected the ancient offence of 'seditious libel' which was banned by the English House of Lords.

The Human Rights Court has repeatedly ruled that governing bodies cannot restrict criticism of themselves and has argued that the term 'protection of the rights of others' does not and can not apply to public bodies.

But the EU and its court, the European Court of Justice, clearly does not regard itself as being bound by the European Convention on Human Rights (which was originally drafted by English lawyers after World War II in order to protect justice and liberty in Europe.) If, astonished by this, you dare to say that the arrogance of EU officials knows no bounds you will be breaking the EU's new law which forbids any criticism of the EU. (I hope it isn't too late to point out that it might be a good idea to read this book in private.)

The EU's new Charter of Fundamental Rights (a remarkable piece of newspeak in itself since it gives the new eurostate rights and takes rights away from individuals) extends its own court's power into the area of civil liberties.

A court which used to deal with single market issues and commercial battles has now been turned into a fully fledged 'we trump all others' supreme court.

There is little doubt that the ECJ will soon rule on free speech cases which involve ordinary EU citizens, eurosceptic parties or eurosceptic publications.

The EU seems determined to take on the Human Rights Court in Strasbourg and to destroy the Convention on Human Rights. It clearly wants to replace the former with its own inappropriately named European Court of Justice and the latter with its own oppressive Charter.

Determined to crush opposition to the idea of a European superstate, the EU has proposed that 'parties which do not respect democratic principles and fundamental rights may be subject to proceedings in the EU court and suspension of their EU funding...'

There is no official definition of 'democratic principles' or 'fundamental rights'.

The Nice Treaty gave the EU the ability to 'lay down criteria for the acceptability of political parties at European level.' (Remember that there soon won't be any other level.)

In case you think this is all theory, remember that the European Union has already illegally boycotted Austria for including members of Georg Haider's party in the Austrian government.

The EU will have the power to withdraw or prevent funding, (private, national or at EU level) for political parties deemed unsuitable. Political parties which do not 'contribute to forming a European awareness' will be forbidden.

Moreover, draft proposals from the EU Commission state that a party must have elected members in at least five EU countries (or have obtained five per cent of the votes in at least five EU countries at the next European elections) before it can be described as a European Political Party.

It is clear from all this that national parties, and parties which criticise the EU, will soon be banned. The EU is beginning to make Stalin's Russia and Mao's China look pretty free and easy to me.

It gets worse. You wouldn't believe it but it does.

The EU can and will interfere if voters elect a political party which the Commission regard as unacceptable. Who says they can do that? They do.

The Council may act if it believes that there is a 'clear risk of a serious breach of fundamental rights'. (There is, of course, no definition of fundamental rights. But it seems clear that any party which opposes the European Federal State will be unacceptable and regarded as breaching fundamental rights.)

In England, the dear old, much-loved Magna Carta and the Bill of Rights gave citizens freedom.

The EU Charter of Human Rights (which, you will remember, now takes precedence over English law) states that: 'the EU may limit all rights and freedoms enumerated in the Charter ... where necessary, in order to meet objectives of general interest recognised by the EU.'

In other words, in future, the individual will only have rights because those rights have been endowed by the State.

And the State (the European State) can take away those rights at will.

And you thought you were a free person?

171

Anyone who supports the EU and the euro is betraying their parents' history and their children's future.

172

In 1963 Charles de Gaulle vetoed England's application to join the Common Market.

This is what he said:

'England is insular. She is maritime. She is linked through her trade, her markets, her supply lines to the most distant countries. She pursues essentially industrial and commercial activities and only slightly agricultural ones. She has, in all her doings, very marked and very original habits and traditions. In short, England's nature, England's structure, England's very situation differs profoundly from those of the continentals.'

How right he was. What a pity our own political leaders did not see this truth as clearly.

173

'Under a government which imprisons any unjustly,
the true place for a just man is also a prison.'
HENRY DAVID THOREAU

174

The European Commission is proposing changes in legislation which will allow drug companies to advertise prescription drugs – for example, those sold for the treatment of disorders as varied as AIDS, asthma and diabetes – directly to the general public. This is yet another piece of legislation planned for no other reason than that it will delight the drug companies. This new legislation will simply lead to a dramatic increase in the number of patients taking unnecessary medication.

175

English abattoirs are still inspected by English meat inspectors, but because of EU regulations the English inspectors have to be supervised by EU experts. Many of the EU experts are so-called 'vets' who have received training lasting just one week. English vets have to undergo training which lasts seven years.

176

When the treaty of Rome was signed in 1957, the ministers representing Germany, Italy and Holland signed blank pieces of paper because the translations of the French original had not been completed.

177

In the EU, bureaucrats now regard themselves as the most important citizens. Despite the fact that these people produce nothing of value their pay and perks packages are extremely generous.

This EU phenomenon has now affected England.

Since New Labour took charge, higher taxes and increased handouts to people receiving state benefits (Labour's main voting block) have done enormous damage to the nation's fiscal fitness. Just as destructive has been the movement of wealth and reward from entrepreneurs and businessmen (who take chances with their futures but whose success creates future employment and economic growth) to civil servants and the thousands of Labour supporters now sitting on quangos.

Under Tony Blair's leadership, civil servants everywhere have received massive pay increases. Middle management council chiefs, hospital administrators and others who have supervised increasing chaos and inefficiency, have received pay rises at least double the inflation rate, and three times those available to workers in the private sector. Top civil servants have had pay rises of 40 to 50 per cent since the year 2000. Health service fat-cat administrators swallow up much of the money promised to the NHS, despite the clear evidence that those running the NHS have made an appalling mess of the job. In addition to massive pay rises, civil servants receive pensions that entrepreneurs and businessmen can only dream of – and perks (such as free houses and free cars) which are virtually unheard of outside state employment circles.

The Government claims that it needs to pay public sector workers more in order to retain good staff. This would be fine if it were true. But it is clearly nonsense. Public sector staff, many of whom are clearly incompetent, now have job security, massive perks and huge pay packets. There is little incentive for anyone to start a new business when they could clearly earn more by getting a safe, undemanding job in local or national government. Would-be entrepreneurs should – and no doubt will – take note.

The danger to the nation is simple. Public officials perform a vital service – it is they who are responsible for ensuring that the infrastructure (transport, hospitals etc.) works well. But public officials don't produce anything and they cost a nation money, rather than adding to its wealth. It is entrepreneurs who create a nation's wealth, who give it prosperity and who must, in the end, pay the salaries of the public officials.

178

If the EU has its way, the England cricket, football and rugby teams will disappear.

179

'MPs are not here to represent their constituencies – they are here to support the new government.'
Tony Blair after his 1997 election win

180

England's history is already being altered and suppressed. It is considered inconvenient and inappropriate for children to know that England fought two wars against Germany. History is being altered to fit in with the EU's plans. England will soon have no history of its own.

181

The EU wants to harmonise VAT throughout Europe for the simple reason that they want more of our money. Part of the VAT we pay already goes directly to Brussels. Now, they want to put VAT on housing, food, medicines, children's clothes, public transport and knowledge in the form of books and magazines.

This harmonisation programme will be easy for the EU's bureaucratic bosses to push through. The EU has already taken charge of VAT rates throughout Europe, and Tony Blair's Labour government has already signed an EU directive putting VAT on houses, books, food etc. (Putting VAT on books, magazines and newspapers will enable the EU bosses to control the dissemination of information more effectively because smaller publishers will go out of business.) The EU also wants to put VAT on credit card transactions and on corporate and personal profits. (This will be added on top of already rising income taxes.)

182

*'Experience should teach us to be most on our guard to protect liberty
when the government's purposes are beneficial. Men born to freedom
are naturally alert to repel invasion of their liberty by evil-minded rulers. The
greatest dangers to liberty lurk in insidious encroachment by men
of zeal, well-meaning but without understanding.'*
USA JUSTICE LOUIS BRANDEIS, 1928

183

The EU clearly needs to harmonise taxes throughout Europe, and despite the firm denials of politicians it has already started to do this. (What a surprise to discover that politicians have not been sharing the whole truth with the people who put them in power.)

Taxes in France and Germany (for a long time these have been high tax countries) have started to come down (much to the delight of their citizens) whereas taxes in England (which were lower) have started to rise at a dramatic rate.

Chancellor Gordon Brown's English Budget 2002 was an EU-friendly budget, and made it clear that the Chancellor has a vision of a world in which we are all to become supplicants of the state. Even families with a combined annual income of £58,000 can now fill in forms to claim benefits intended for the poor.

Brown would, I suspect, like to take charge of every pay packet, dividend cheque and inheritance and then dole out 'pocket money' as and how he sees fit. That is the EU way.

When Labour took power in 1997, the state took 38 per cent of England's wealth. Under Brown the take has risen to 42 per cent – very close to the average take in Europe. And there is the clue. Tax rises in England were predictable, inevitable and essential. Tax rates throughout the rest of Europe have been falling in recent years but rising in England and there is a simple explanation for this.

If Europe is to have a single Government and a single tax rate it is essential that individual countries have tax rates which are close to one another. Too much variation from country to country would make it impossible to introduce a unified tax structure. The Labour Government has made it clear that the recent tax hike is just the start and that taxes in England will continue to rise as long as the Labour Party remains in power. Tony Blair and his incompetent colleagues are 'tax and spend' politicians. Although they have proved themselves quite incapable of running anything, they think they know best how to spend the voters' money. England's future gets gloomier by the day. The evidence shows that even modest tax rises prevent entrepreneurs from setting up new businesses. Allied with the miles of red-tape introduced by the EU-friendly Labour party, these extra taxes will, before long, lead to inflation, high interest rates and an economic depression.

In 1997, the English paid £286 billion in tax. By 2001, under Labour's stewardship, the tax take had risen to £370 billion. Most of this extra tax has gone not to help English businesses, improve education or boost the NHS. It has, instead, gone to the EU or into social security payments. In 1997, the English Government paid out £76 billion in social security payments. By 2001, the figure was up to £111 billion – a dramatic, way above inflation, pay rise. A massive 38 per cent of English families now receive a means tested benefit. The only true beneficiary of all this largesse with the taxpayers' funds will be the Labour Party at the next election when happy recipients will be expected to repay Blair and Brown by putting an X under the name of the local Labour candidate. (If a good chunk of those voters feel obliged – or spurred by self interest – to vote for the party which has so dramatically increased their benefits then the Labour Party will never be voted out of office. Blair and Brown may well have discovered the secret of permanent power.) It is hardly surprising that millions of English citizens have already emigrated, and now live outside England.

The English Government's demands for tax revenue continue to rise at an astonishing rate – though, thanks to Blair and Brown's infinite capacity for slyness, many of the taxes are 'hidden' or 'indirect'.

In England, the Government has massively increased its net receipts in the last five years.

England's total tax burden – which was one of the lowest in the world when Blair took over – is now one of the highest. Despite this massive increase in tax the Labour Government is heading for serious debt. The appalling Byers Railtrack fiasco in late 2001 seems certain to increase the cost of Government borrowing. Blair claims that taxes will have to rise to improve the NHS. But the truth is that taxes will have to rise to help pay for the Government's wastefulness and bad management. The NHS does not need, and will not receive, the additional money raised through higher taxation.

When New Labour came to power in 1997, the Government's income (the tax revenue) was £286 billion (approximately £4,700 per head of population in England). In 2002, the Government took £400 billion in tax (equivalent to around £6,600 per head). Top rate tax in England is now, effectively, 47.5 per cent. Anyone running their own business pays a top rate of 53.8 per cent. Englishmen and Englishwomen are now paying £4 in tax for every £3 they paid when New Labour took power.

By the year 2006 (when Labour's second Parliament will come to an end) the tax take will total at least £473 billion. (That is £7,900 per head). If Labour introduces any additional taxes (and it is a safe bet that there will be tax rises in the next budget) the amount taken will be even greater.

Within one decade, Labour will have managed to double the amount of tax on English citizens.

If New Labour are unable to restrain their greed, or to find a way to overcome their incompetence, they will overshoot and end up charging more in tax than any other European country – that will probably mean charging more tax than any other country in the world. (The cynics might say that England will then at least find one table it can head.)

184

The French make up many of the EU rules and organise the EU bureaucracy. They then ignore the EU rules and the EU bureaucrats whenever it suits them. (Somehow they also always seem to manage to take more cash out of the EU than they put in.)

185

When asked for my nationality these days I always say 'English'. Never just 'British'.

186

*'The issue today is the same as it has been throughout all history; whether
man shall be allowed to govern himself or be ruled by a small elite.'*
THOMAS JEFFERSON

187

In Europe, the law doesn't matter, and being right doesn't matter
either. What does matter is who you know, and having influence
and money. 'The law is something we apply to our enemies. For
our friends we interpret it,' admitted a former Italian prime minister.
An astonishing number of European politicians should be in prison.
No wonder New Labour feels comfortable working with the EU.

188

The EU's path to power has been exactly the same as Hitler's;
using the law (apparently convincingly and with good purpose),
taking power bit by bit and making decisions quickly and without
public discussion.

189

'We have not abolished slavery; we have nationalised it.'
HERBERT SPENCER

190

Where is the accountability within the EU? No one ever takes
responsibility for errors or incompetence.

191

New EU copyright laws are so absurd that there is a good chance
that they will make it illegal to view websites.
    Other EU countries will ignore such a law – rightly regarding it
as too nonsensical to take seriously.

However, the chances are that officials in England will take it just as seriously as they take other nonsensical EU laws.

192

'The last time Britain went into Europe with any degree of success was on 6th June 1944.'
DAILY EXPRESS, 1980

193

In the summer of 2002 it was announced that Romano Prodi, the European Commission president, wants to create an inner core of 'fewer than 10' vice presidents. His plan is for his new inner cabinet (consisting of himself and his vice presidents) to meet at least once a week. This small group of unelected, unaccountable officials will then run the new eurostate.

194

Here's another perfect example for those who doubt that we now live in a fascist tyranny. Taxpayers' money is being used to teach children to support the EU.

195

What sort of democracy do we live in where government officials ignore their responsibilities to the citizens and enforce laws (such as metrication) that the people don't want?

196

If England enters the euro there will be no going back. It will be a terrible mistake which no one will ever be able to put right. Selling England to the EU is such a betrayal that beside it cronyism, crookery, deceit, the Dome and the backhanders fade into insignificance.

197

*'Must the citizen ever for a moment, or in the least degree, resign his
conscience to the legislator? Why has every man a conscience then? I
think that we should be men first, and subjects afterwards. It is not
desirable to cultivate a respect for the law, so much as for the right.
The only obligation which I have the right to assume, is to do at
any time what I think right. Law never made men a whit more just;
and by means of their respect for it, even the well disposed are
daily made the agents of injustice.'*
HENRY DAVID THOREAU

198

For years now the EU has spent over £1 billion a year on supporting the production of poor quality tobacco – poisonous and therefore rather unsuitable for sale in Europe and which must be
'dumped' on undeveloped countries. Many Greek farmers exist on
these grants, as indeed do many French and Spanish farmers. Many
of these farmers have given up other crops because the grants for
tobacco growing are so generous. I first exposed this scandal ten
years ago but nothing has changed. Even if the tobacco was high
quality just what is the EU doing subsidising tobacco growers?

199

Two Dozen Great English Inventors/Discoverers

Charles Babbage (computer)
John Baskerville (type)
Roger Bacon (magnifying glasses, spectacles, telescopes, gunpowder,
flying machines)
Richard Arkwright (spinning frame)
John Fleming (vacuum diode)
William Henry Fox Talbot (photography)
Robert Hooke (universal joint)
Frank Whittle (jet propulsion)
William Henry Perkin (synthetic dyes)
Michael Faraday (dynamo)

Edmund Halley (diving bell)
Earl of Sandwich (sandwich)
Thomas Saint (sewing machine)
John Walker (friction match)
Rowland Hill (postage stamp)
Isaac Newton (reflecting telescopes)
Joseph Bramah (hydraulic press)
Francis Pettit Smith (propeller)
George Stephenson (the first locomotive)
Christopher Cockerell (hovercraft)
Alexander Fleming (penicillin)
Joseph Lister (antiseptic surgery)
Tim Berners-Lee (the World Wide Web)
Edwin Budding (lawnmower)

200

England will not collapse if we leave the EU. Small countries do very well outside the bureaucratic stranglehold of the EU. Iceland has 275,000 citizens and survives very well without faceless wimps in Brussels telling it what to do. Greenland left the EU. Switzerland and Norway (both smaller than England) said 'no' and do magnificently. There are almost 50 countries in Europe. Less than a third of them are in the EU. The EU is for losers which cannot cope alone. England is not a loser.

201

'Above all, the EEC takes away Britain's freedom to follow the economic policies we need. We will negotiate withdrawal from the EEC which has drained our natural resources and destroyed our jobs.'
TONY BLAIR 1982/3

202

Everyone who isn't on a State payroll (either as a civil servant or welfare recipient) is being taxed to death (and then taxed after it too).

203

For an English business with up to 10 members of staff, the cost of complying with Government red tape went up from £3,600 in the year 2000 to £4,100 in 2001. For a small business with up to 50 employees, the cost of complying with red tape was £8,000 in the year 2000 and £10,100 in the year 2001. For bigger companies, the cost of all the new regulations becomes really scary. For a company with more than 50 employees, the cost of dealing with government bureaucracy was 25 per cent higher in 2001 than it was in 2000. Astonishingly, one in every 15 private sector employees in England is now working full time trying to sort out paperwork introduced by Gordon Brown and the EU-influenced New Labour government. With help from New Labour, the EU is killing English industry at quite a pace.

204

When the EU began it was decided that everything permitted should be written down, and everything not written down should not be permitted. Hence we have the absurdity of regulations such as the EU directive on duck eggs. This nonsense (of which the Marx Brothers would have been proud) runs to 26,911 words. By comparison the American Declaration of Independence is just 1,300 words. The Ten Commandments and Abraham Lincoln's Gettysburg address are around 300 words each.

205

Many modern European politicians want power, wealth and fame for life. They are terrified of ending up like their predecessors – sad old has-beens, living on speeches and books of memoirs, with no power, no respect and little money.

206

Germany has played its EU membership very cleverly. The Germans, unlike other Europeans, have kept themselves an opt out clause if things go wrong. The 16 provincial governments within Germany control most things within their regions. The federal German government cannot act without unanimous approval from the 16. The 16 German provinces have never signed any agreement with the EU. It was the federal German government which signed up. If things go badly wrong the individual regions can leave the EU.

207

In 1993, when the Danish people rejected the Maastricht Treaty, they were made to vote again. They were told that they would have to keep voting until they got it right. Does this remind you of anything? The Soviet Union perhaps? In the final referendum the Danes were asked to vote 'yes' for four opt-outs to the Maastricht treaty. The Danish people duly did this, because they didn't like these clauses. Their Government interpreted these 'no' votes as a 'yes' vote for the treaty as a whole, but with the four opt-outs. (Any 'no' votes for the four opt outs were interpreted as a 'yes' to the whole treaty without the opt outs being removed.) There was no way to vote 'no' to the Maastricht treaty.

208

In 1997, Germany had less than £5 billion worth of gold tucked away in its vaults. By 1999, the Germans had somehow managed to accumulate over £20 billion worth of gold.

Just how they managed this is something of a mystery.

Now, here's a thought.

It is no secret that the German people don't like the euro. They liked the deutschmark and they miss it terribly.

If the Germans decide to abandon the euro (a not unlikely scenario) they will naturally re-launch the deutschmark. They will be able to underpin their re-launched currency with gold. Other EU countries will not be able to do this. Consequently, other EU countries will have to accept the deutschmark as their currencies too.

The Germans would then have total control of the European Bank and the EU.

Just a thought.

209

The EU working time directive (which makes a maximum 35 hour week compulsory) will be applied to everyone originally exempt – including doctors, cab drivers, fishermen and the self-employed. The batty bureaucrats of Brussels who thought up the 35 hour week (and, presumably, welcomed it themselves) believed that with their staff working fewer hours, companies would have to hire more employees – and therefore reduce unemployment levels. Unfortunately, the batty bureaucrats have so little experience of real life that they did not realise that their new law would reduce profits so much that many companies would simply go bust and have to fire everyone. Many businesses which have survived have had to lay off staff to pay for the 35 hour week.

The end result is that this EU nonsense hasn't created any real new jobs at all. The only new jobs have been for bureaucrats hired to help out the bureaucrats who are now at their desks for a maximum of 35 hours a week, and to keep an eye on private and public companies to make sure they obey the daft new rules. Incidentally, the EU working hours directive isn't helping the NHS. Nurses and other staff are having to be supplemented with expensive agency staff.

210

Anyone who opposes the EU is described as a fascist. But that is a barefaced lie.

The official Oxford English Dictionary definition of a fascist is: 'One of a body of Italian nationalists organised in 1919 under Benito Mussolini to oppose Bolshevism.'

Now, this, admittedly, doesn't take us much further forward so the next step is to see how Mussolini, the 'inventor' of this political philosophy (and the ultimate lamp-post decoration) defined fascism. And this is where it gets interesting.

Here is Mussolini's definition: 'Liberalism denied the state in the name of the individual; fascism reasserts the rights of the state as expressing the real essence of the individual.'

Read that and remember that Mussolini invented fascism. His definition is, by definition, unarguably correct. Mussolini's views on most things may well be best brushed under the carpet. But his views on fascism are the very best. Fascism was, after all, a topic on which the man was an expert. If Mussolini had gone in for Mastermind his chosen subject would have been fascism and he would have scored top marks.

And you don't need to think about Mussolini's definition for long to realise that the European Union is a fundamentally fascist state.

211

Remember: France, Italy, Germany and Spain are still funding generous state pensions out of general taxation. They need your pension savings.

212

Don't comfort yourself with the thought that within the EU, England can vote against anything it doesn't like. Majority voting is now a fact of life. The EU can decide things for us and there isn't a thing we can do about it if we don't like their new rules.

Successive Governments have handed over more and more power.

Indeed, if we choose not to join the euro the EU can decide for us – forcing us to join whether we want to or not.

213

The sole legitimate function of a government is to protect the rights of its citizens.

That is why governments were created. It is why they exist. There is no other reason. A government only has a right to tax the people in order to pursue that simple aim. It does not have the right to raise taxes if it intends to waste that money or, worse still, to use the money to oppress the citizens. It does not have the right to raise money through taxation when that money will be used to push through legislation which takes away the citizen's freedom.

But how many of the things our Government – and the EU – do are done to protect the right to life, liberty and the pursuit of happiness?

Just look at what citizens everywhere have a right to expect from their Government – and how our Government is failing in its duty.

1. Citizens have a right to be able to walk the streets safely – day or night. But there are very few towns in England today where it is safe for a law-abiding citizen to walk after 10 p.m.

2. Citizens have a right to know that their politicians will keep their promises. If politicians don't keep their electoral promises what is the point in voting for them? Blair & Co. have lied and cheated endlessly. As a result, most people won't bother to vote at the next election – and that will suit Blair just fine.

3. Citizens have a right to live their lives freely and in privacy. But Blair & Co. have steadily removed freedoms and the right to privacy. English citizens are losing their status as citizens and rapidly becoming serfs in Blairdom.

4. Citizens have a right to know that their Government will protect them when they are on foreign soil. But the evidence shows that our Government will not protect English citizens when they are abroad. The elected Prime Minister is more concerned with helping the Americans than looking after the people who pay his wages.

5. Citizens have a right to know that our taxes are used only for essential and approved public services – and that our money is not wasted. Blair's Government has wasted billions of pounds of taxpayers' hard earned money. Vast quantities of cash have been frittered away on absurdly expensive wallpaper, the pointless Dome, personal servants and vast numbers of spin doctors.

6. Citizens have a right to be able to travel around their country freely and safely. The English now have a transport system which is one of the worst in the world. Train travel has become an expensive lottery with no prizes. Road travel is slow and hazardous. The police are more concerned with collecting speeding fines than with keeping traffic moving safely.

7. Citizens have a right to know that they will be able to find good health care when and where they need it. But health care in England is a constantly deteriorating shambles. The Government has given up and is now paying to send a few selected patients abroad for treatment.

8.   Citizens have a right to know that their Government will pro-
      tect their savings and investments. But the Government itself
      stole billions from small savers by stealing Railtrack from its
      shareholders.
9.   Citizens have a right to know that their Government will
      provide decent education for their children. But the level of
      illiteracy in England is rising dramatically. Schools are dismal.
      Teachers are demoralised. There is little discipline or learning.
10.   Citizens have a right to clean drinking water and to be able to
      buy good quality food at reasonable prices.
11.   Citizens have a right to know that the taxes they are charged
      will be fair and that the money raised will be used for the
      benefit of the community.
12.   Citizens have a right to know that their security and freedom
      will be protected by a fair system of justice – with honest po-
      licemen and courts administering justice fairly. This we do
      not have.

Citizens everywhere have a right to expect their Government to
set an example: to be honest, honourable and fair in its dealings.
But the English have a Government which is dishonest, dishonour-
able and unfair.

Any government exists to make its citizens' lives better and freer.
That is what it is there for. Politicians are paid well, and given
numerous perks, in order to provide their employers (the electorate) with good government.

But in what way has the Blair government (now well into its
second term and therefore no longer able to blame the previous
government for everything that goes wrong) contributed to the freedom and well-being of English citizens?

If a company fails to fulfil its promises to its customers it will be
hauled into court. Why are Blair and his wretched companions
immune to the law?

It is the duty of those in government to behave responsibly and
in the public interest. But most of those in government now are too
conceited, too arrogant and too concerned with their own personal
futures to put the public interest anywhere near the top of their
personal agenda.

It is hardly surprising that the exodus of English citizens, leaving to live abroad, now far exceeds the number of alleged asylum seekers arriving in England to take advantage of the free benefits system. (Although, for the record, most asylum seekers don't use the English health service – they go back home when they need medical treatment).

We have accepted all this because we do not see an alternative.

Blair's Government is the most uncaring, irresponsible and dishonest of my lifetime, though I doubt if the Conservatives or Liberals would do a better job. That is the shame of modern politicians.

It is our silent acquiescence which enables Blair to cheat us in this way. That is our shame.

The easiest thing to do is nothing.

The easy way out is to turn our backs; to console ourselves with the thought that we can do nothing to change the way things are.

And if we choose to do that then we can hardly complain if things continue to get worse: if our freedoms and privacy and rights continue to disappear and our leaders continue to treat us without respect.

But should we really allow them to continue to get away with their arrogance and their deceit?

We have been betrayed by a bunch of greedy, uncaring, deceitful men and women who are concerned only with their own careers.

Blair has cheated the public. New Labour has put up taxes dramatically but has invested far too little in new hospitals, schools and roads.

Where did all the money go?

Blair and his wastrel chums spent it on spin doctors, parties and fancy wallpaper. But most of all they gave it away to EU bureaucrats.

As a result we now live in the worst and feeblest 'developed' country in the world.

If we do nothing England under Blair will soon become a Third World country.

We need to act together. We need to take back our country from the no-hopers who are running it into the ground.

Look up the word 'kakistocracy' in the dictionary. It means 'the government of a state by the worst citizens'. And that is what we've got. We're living in a kakistocracy.

We do not have to give in and let our world be ruined by unimaginative, second rate citizens.

Together we can do anything we want to do.

How many marks out of ten would you give your Government for honesty, decency, caring, efficiency?

214

The new European army, containing 60,000 soldiers, will soon replace the English army – with all its traditions. The soldiers in it will speak heaven knows how many different languages and the result will, inevitably, be chaos. What was once the English army will no longer be free to do anything (even defend England) unless bureaucrats in Brussels give the go ahead. The new EU army could even be used against the English people if there was a rebellion against the EU.

215

'I do verily believe that ... a single, consolidated government would become the most corrupt government on the earth.'
THOMAS JEFFERSON

216

The EU does three things well. It puts up costs, increases bureaucracy and reduces genuine employment possibilities. We need the EU like we need more politicians.

217

According to a survey published in the *International Herald Tribune*, barely half of all citizens in EU member countries trust the EU.

218

Around 20 per cent of the money paid to the EU is stolen or wasted.

219

'Germany as the biggest and most powerful economic member state will be the leader (of Europe) whether you like it not.'
THEO WAIGEL, FORMER GERMAN FINANCE MINISTER, 1997

220

The remains of democracy as we know it will disappear by 2009 when there will be European candidates for the European Parliament. The European candidates will represent the Federation of European countries. National political parties will cease to exist. Voters will vote for a party not an individual. There will be no opposition. Just the European Federation candidates. That's just seven years away. What does it remind you of? What's that big country to the east? Lots of snow.

Meanwhile, all citizens of countries in the EU are already 'citizens of the union' and subject to the duties imposed thereby. What are the duties? What are your obligations?

No one knows. They have never been defined. Our leaders have signed away our rights in an open contract – without even telling us, let alone asking for our views.

Mind you, I expect you'll find out what your obligations are when you break one.

(Did your MP or MEP tell you any of this when they last stuffed a leaflet through your letter box?)

221

The state of the EU is, we are constantly being told, far more important than our heritage, our history or our individuality. What the EU wants the EU must get – regardless of the cost to us as citizens. That is fascism.

We are repeatedly told that we must sacrifice our freedom and our independence so that the state can grow stronger.

That, let me remind you, is exactly what fascism is.

There is no little irony in the fact that anyone who wants their country to leave the EU these days is automatically labelled a right wing extremist, a fascist and a racist.

The European leaders who enthusiastically promote the interests of the EU above their nation's individual interests are dyed in the wool fascists.

And that's the raw truth. It happened slowly and without the polishing of jackboots or the giving of silly salutes but we already live in a fascist state.

It's here. It's happened. And there is something surreal and unpleasantly 'emperor's new clothesish' about the fact that EU politicians are now screaming at us to warn us that nationalists, who want to preserve tradition and freedom, are fascists.

222

'Smile at us, pay us, pass us; but do not quite forget.
For we are the people of England, that never have spoken yet.'
G.K. CHESTERTON

223

English nursing homes are going into receivership faster than ever. This is putting enormous pressure on NHS hospitals because there is nowhere for elderly patients to go to – even when they no longer need hospital care. Nursing homes are being destroyed by pointless new EU regulations (and unnecessary form filling).

224

'When we build the house of Europe the future will belong to Germany.'
HELMUT KOHL (GERMAN POLITICIAN)

225

Children are being taught that the EU is essential for England's future and that the euro offers the nation's only chance of future security. Both these claims are lies – but even if they were true these are issues which need to be discussed not simply fed into young minds through indoctrination. The EU gives grants to areas where children are properly indoctrinated about the value of the EU.

226

European countries have nothing to hold them together. They have nothing in common; no common language; no common culture; no common view of things; no common destiny. Why try to unite such a varied group of nations? What is the point? Diversity is best. And yet the EU bureaucrats want us all to be the same. There are 360,000,000 people living in the EU countries. The Greeks have very little in common with the Germans. The Italians have nothing in common with the Irish.

And yet a handful of bureaucrats think they can control them with regulations. Nothing in common, no passion. Just rules and regulations. Make you think of anything? USSR?

227

'This royal throne of kings, this sceptred isle,
This earth of majesty, this seat of Mars,
This other Eden, demi-paradise,
This fortress built by Nature for herself
Against infection and the hand of war,
This happy breed of men, this little world,
This precious stone set in the silver sea,
Which serves it in the office of a wall,
Or as a moat defensive to a house,
Against the envy of less happier lands;
This blessed plot, this earth, this realm, this England,
This nurse, this teeming womb of royal kings,
Fear'd by their breed, and famous by their birth.'
WILLIAM SHAKESPEARE

228

I am not against 'Europe'. On the contrary I love it. I love the variety – the unique qualities which make France France, Holland Holland, Germany Germany and Italy Italy. It is the variety which I love about these European countries. Spain is different to Austria in every imaginable way. There are differences within Germany but the differences between Germany and Spain are far greater than any of those internal differences. When Europe has become a single state those international differences will gradually disappear. The politicians and bureaucrats planning the new eurostate are clearly determined to destroy individual national characteristics – that is why they are making sure that the new regions cross over traditional national boundaries.

I want the variety to stay. I don't want those individual identities to disappear into a new, one-fits-all superstate. I don't want England, France and Italy to be just regions within the new Europe.

229

'Why does Europe need fifteen foreign ministers when one is enough?
Why do member states still need national armies?
One European army is enough.'
HANS EICHEL (GERMAN FINANCE MINISTER NOV 1999)

230

A European police force, operating under EU laws, has now been formed.

There will now be no need for extradition processes because Europol will have rights across national borders.

Astonishingly, even the EU Parliament seems alarmed at the powers of Europol.

In a report entitled *Police and Justice in the EU*, the Parliament described Europol as: 'the emergence of an embryonic federal system of repression, the creation of a federal police (Europol), a federal prosecutor (Eurojust) and a concept of federal crimes or Eurocrimes. All the agents of these departments would have immunity from prosecution.'

Like much else in Europe, Europol does not seem to be overseen by any democratic body. The buildings, offices and archives of the Europol offices cannot be investigated or entered. They are above the law. In April 2001, Europol even refused to submit to scrutiny by the EU Parliament.

The EU Parliament, throwing a justifiable moody, described Europol as a 'repressive monster'.

And then there is Eurojust.

I don't know what Eurojust is because it has undefined powers. However, I do know that Eurojust, despite its name, will never defend – only prosecute on behalf of the new European superstate.

What was the name of that book by George Orwell?

231

Three Dozen Great English Writers

William Shakespeare
Charles Dickens
P.G. Wodehouse
Evelyn Waugh
Lewis Carroll
Anthony Trollope
Samuel Johnson
George Eliot
Jane Austen
Charlotte Brontë (& Anne and Emily)
Henry Fielding
Daniel Defoe
Virgina Woolf
Charles Lamb
R.D. Blackmore
H.G. Wells
Arnold Bennett
Rudyard Kipling
John Bunyan
Anthony Burgess
John Ruskin
William Makepeace Thackeray
Algernon Charles Swinburne
Percy Bysshe Shelley
D.H. Lawrence
Alexander Pope
Graham Greene
Aldous Huxley
George Orwell

Ben Jonson
G.K. Chesterton
Noel Coward
Agatha Christie
William Morris
Wilkie Collins
T.H. White

232

Right wing extremist parties – with xenophobic policies – are gaining more and more power in Europe as a result of the EU.

It's happening in England and it's happening in Germany, France, Austria, Belgium and Italy. Soldiers in the German army celebrated Hitler's birthday with Nazi salutes.

The introduction of the euro, and the attempt to turn Europe into a single bureaucratic nation, is responsible for this rise in xenophobia – a development which could easily turn into widespread genuine racism.

The Germans and the French are becoming increasingly embittered at the prospect of seeing their hard-won prosperity diluted as their nations are subjugated to a monolithic State.

Racism could quickly spread throughout Europe as more and more people become angry at what is happening to their country.

The best way to stop the development of racism is to abandon the EU superstate.

233

'Power without responsibility – the prerogative of the harlot throughout the ages.'
RUDYARD KIPLING

234

Do you remember the petrol protests in England during the autumn of 2000? Long queues at the pumps. Tanker drivers in disputes. All sorts of accusations and counter accusations.

Blair and Brown stood firm and refused to lower petrol taxes.

Or did they?

In fact, two weeks before the protest, Brown had attended a meeting of the European Council of Ministers where the EU had decided that England's petrol tax would not be reduced.

Blair and Brown had no choice. They did what they were told. There are other examples of Europe interfering with the English tax system.

For example, in his pre-budget speech in November 2000, Gordon Brown announced that he was cutting the tax on repairs to church buildings to five per cent.

Oh, no you aren't Gordon.

The EU ordered that the churches should pay the full 17.5 per cent rate and Brown was overruled.

235

'There's always something fishy about the French.'
NOEL COWARD

236

So, what does Blair get out of the EU? Permanent power. He can move into an unelected position. Today, the lines between elected and unelected are blurred but the unelected have more power. Kinnock and Patten, both failed politicians, rejected by the English people, now have more power as Commissioners than they would ever had even if they had been elected. That is the future which Blair is buying for himself. The price is England.

237

If England joins the euro it will mean handing over control of our interest rates (and therefore house prices and employment levels) to the EU bank in Germany. If England joins the euro we're acknowledging that World War I and World War II were a waste of lives. We could have saved ourselves effort and bloodshed by joining Hitler in 1939. Those desperate to hand over our sovereignty to the EU won't tell you that – but it's the truth.

238

The English Parliament's European Select Committee processes 1,000 documents a year and does this in meetings which last for around half an hour a week.

239

We have allowed the EU to take away our self sufficiency. Many English homes are now supplied with water and electricity which is sold to them by companies owned in France or Germany.

240

'The right most valued by all civilised men is the right to be left alone..'
US SUPREME COURT JUSTICE LOUIS BRANDEIS

241

The last inappropriate alliance of nations was the USSR. Remember what happened to that? The EU is a crisis waiting to happen.

242

Joining the euro won't be the beginning of something wonderful. It will be the end of England; the end of everything you know, love and respect.

243

Politicians keen for England to join the euro include Stephen Byers, Robin Cook and Peter Mandelson.

244

The system of proportional representation (favoured in the EU) may, on the surface, sound fairer than England's old-fashioned first-past-the-post system.

But the party list system of proportional representation favoured by the EU – means that professional politicians can stay in power for ever – without having to worry about being elected.

Citizens give their votes to a party, not a politician. And the people who control the party decide which politicians get the seats, the salaries, the houses, the cars, the pensions and the perks.

New boundaries for the European Parliament elections reduce the number of constituencies dramatically. In future, each constituency will have between 3 and 11 MEPs – all nominated by the leaders of the various political parties. It will be impossible to vote for an individual MEP (unless you vote for a true independent).

You will simply be expected to vote for a party. And since all the main parties support the EU there is little opportunity for dissent.

245

At all recent English elections, all three major political parties have been pro-EU so there hasn't been much choice on the big issue.

246

'Politics is the art of preventing people from taking part in affairs which properly concern them.'
PAUL VALERY

247

Some time ago, Germany made loans to the former USSR. These loans were originally guaranteed by the German Bundesbank but are now guaranteed by the European Central Bank. The value of the loans is believed to be around £130 billion. As members of the EU we are now jointly responsible for that debt, and we are paying for the natural gas now supplied to Germany from the former USSR. Cynical observers might wonder if Germany could have deliberately built up huge debts – knowing that these would be taken over by the EU.

248

English citizens used to be able to petition their Monarch if they had a concern or grievance. This right was given under the Magna Carta. According to the law of England the House of Lords must accept petitions from citizens, and take them to the reigning Monarch. The Monarch must then hear them.

This right has now been quietly set aside. Petitions raised by citizens now go to the relevant minister and are invariably simply shredded.

The Magna Carta, signed by King John in June 1215, still stands. It is doubtful if even the fat burghers of Brussels can make it go away.

Much of what has been done in recent years is undoubtedly illegal, unconstitutional and contrary to both English common law and the Magna Carta.

So, why not test the legality of EU legislation in court?
You can't.

Try it, and you will be dismissed as a 'vexatious litigant'. The courts will not even hear the case. Ministers and the EU regard themselves as being above the law – and out of the reach of ordinary citizens. When I recently tried to take the Home Secretary to court (for stomping on my human rights and my freedom to speak out) I was told that I could not.

We have taxation without representation.

249

'The Almighty in His infinite wisdom did not see fit to create Frenchmen in the image of Englishmen.'
WINSTON CHURCHILL

250

By the year 2004, foreign fishing fleets will be allowed to fish right up to the English shoreline. England's six and twelve mile coastal territorial limits will be abolished.

251

Today, the English fishing industry spends £108 million a year enforcing regulations from the EU. The effect of this can be judged by the fact that the entire fishing industry is only worth £600 million.

252

In recent years, fishing vessels from other EU countries have been given special permission to pick up cod swimming to spawn in English waters, while English fishermen, who have traditionally fished the waters around the English coastline, have been instructed by the EU to stay in port – even though their boats and nets are smaller. There is no logical explanation for this.

253

According to the European Commission England is now Europe's most bureaucratic nation.

The Chamber of Commerce estimates that red tape has cost English firms over £15.6 billion in the last four years.

The CBI claims that the Government introduces an average of ten new regulations every day each year.

It is, quite clearly, now utterly impossible for anyone to keep up with this torrent of new legislation. Even companies which have full-time compliance officers find it impossible to find their way around the laws. (Actually, even civil servants find it impossible to keep up with regulations brought in by other departments.)

Entrepreneurs starting businesses or running small businesses which do not justify the employment of a full-time compliance officer have absolutely no chance of satisfying all the legal requirements.

Part of the problem is undoubtedly the fact that endless new European rulings are incorporated into English law but instead of replacing existing law they are simply added onto English laws. Old laws are never repealed. The final result is mass confusion. Only the lawyers benefit. (The Blairs are both lawyers.)

254

Maybe the English should organise a management buy-out to escape from the EU.

255

It has been reported that in an interview with an American journalist, British PM Tony Blair, referring to those citizens who want England to remain independent, with its own laws, own Parliament and own currency commented: 'If that is the sort of country people want to live in, then fuck them.'

256

The real power in the EU is held by the members of the EC – the appointed Commissioners. Just how they are chosen is something of a secret. Secrecy and power by appointment is now the norm in Europe. Many of the powerful people at the European Central Bank are political appointees – some of them former politicians with no experience of banking. The EU judiciary is unelected, and unaccountable and has given itself the power to create new laws. Many of these new laws seem designed to protect the EU, regardless of the cost to individuals.

257

Critics of the EU are often accused of 'racism'.

The EU's defenders use this as a term of abuse because they know that it will frighten people. No one wants to be thought to be a 'racist' (any more than they want to be known as a 'fascist').

Anyone who fights for their own national interests, or who wants to defend their family or community, is automatically and rather sneeringly dismissed as being a 'racist'.

All European leaders who can be described as 'nationalists' have been monstered as 'fascists' and 'racists' and distinctly unsavoury.

It has become politically correct (and not in the slightest bit racist) to hold prejudices against white, middle-class, working Christians. If they are English then all the better. Even white, middle-class, English, Christian politicians (particularly the male ones) feel that they are duty bound to observe and sanctify these prejudices.

Ambition, drive and respect are no longer virtues; they are, rather, regarded as unsavoury; indications of something almost murky and disrespectable. There is an open season for those who wish to attack the middle-classes. Even the courts are joining in. Defend your home, express any sort of opinion, try to protect your family or earn a living and you will be persecuted by a seemingly endless variety of self-important authorities. Try selling apples by the pound and see just how quickly you attract the attention of nasty little petty-minded bureaucrats in cheap suits. They lurk in dark corners; institutional cockroaches ever looking for the exceptional, the entrepreneurial or, Brussels forbid, the eccentric.

Racism is the belief that a particular race is superior to all others. Being a nationalist does not mean that you are a racist. Wanting to protect your heritage, your identity, your community and your beliefs does not mean that you are a racist. I don't believe that being English makes me better (or worse) than a German, Belgian, Frenchman or Italian. But I do believe I am entitled to be proud of my 'Englishness' and I refuse to apologise for it or to be ashamed of it. Why is it not acceptable for an Englishman to describe himself as an English nationalist? During the Football World Cup in 2002, supporters in England were told to take down their English flags on the grounds that the flags might upset people of other nationalities. But foreigners, supporting their teams, were not told to take down their flags. That, presumably, would have been regarded as racist by the politically correct. I wonder if the authorities would have dared order people to take down an EU flag. (Assuming, of course, that anyone had wanted to put one up.)

Blair and his dangerous EU allies redefine words in their own interests. We are, like Alice, living in a Wonderland where words mean whatever the politicians want them to mean.

The EU apologists believe that it is racist to care about your family, your community and your country. I don't. Is it racist to believe that it would be wise not to welcome new immigrants (wherever they are from and whatever their skin colour may be) until your country can provide jobs and a basic level of health care for its existing citizens? Is it racist for the English to object to Americans and Europeans being able to take advantage of our free NHS when the English have to pay for health care if they travel to other countries? If you don't define a problem how are you ever going to solve it? Hiding from the truth, describing the truth as 'racist', does no good at all.

Blair believes (or seems to believe) that it is racist to care about your heritage, your nation, your history. That isn't what racism is at all.

258

'It is not in the nature of things that a central government should be able to watch over all the needs of a great nation. Decentralisation is the chief cause of the substantial progress we have made in civilisation.'
ALEXIS DE TOCQUEVILLE

259

European law is not designed or put into action by European politicians but by 23,000 unelected bureaucrats of the EC.

These bureaucrats have enormous power. Their laws become law when they say so and individual parliaments, representing member countries, have no real authority any more.

The European Court of Justice has ruled that a directive must come into force on the due date even if it hasn't been incorporated into a nation's law.

If a national parliament should have the courage to reject an EU law, that law will be imposed. (This has already happened in Denmark.)

260

The EU has been compared to the former Soviet Union. There is a council of ministers (the ruling clique), the European Commission (the politburo) and a parliament (the supreme soviet). The rulers are unaccountable to the people and contemptuous of them. The people with the power can't be fired or changed or held to account by the people. The EU introduces laws which bind its successors and cannot be repealed; it creates laws by directive, without any regard for the needs and rights of businesses or individuals. And the EU gathers around it 'satellite' or weaker states – promising them membership of the EU in due course.

261

According to Ashley Mote, in his book *Vigilance,* Lord Tebbit reports that when he was Trade Minister, the EU wanted him to bring in a working time directive (similar to the one now in existence). He said they could introduce it in the EU but that he wasn't introducing it in England. The EU's representatives complained that that would leave England with a competitive advantage. Tebbit then pointed out that the EU spokesmen had spent all morning arguing that the working time directive was necessary for efficiency and competitiveness.

The truth, of course, is that the EU just wanted to shackle the English with rules which they themselves could ignore.

Eventually, Blair's government pushed through the working time directive (which controls the number of hours employees can work). This EU legislation, which costs English businesses around £2 billion a year, was pushed through Parliament on the day before the summer recess with no time for proper debate.

262

The European Parliament is a farce. On one occasion, 287 votes were taken in just over an hour. No one can really know what they are voting for or against. They merely press buttons. When an MEP felt the voting was disorganised and dishonest (over an EU budget of around £65 billion) he protested that no one had a clue what was going on and the paperwork did not relate to the voting. But no record of his protest appeared anywhere. The criticism was edited out because it was considered embarrassing and inconvenient.

In the European Parliament, MEPs who are absent are presumed to have voted in favour of every resolution. Their votes are duly counted in support of each motion which they miss.

263

The EU desperately want to keep England locked safely in the EU not because they love us and want us in their club but because they want to reduce our competitive advantage in trading with the rest of the world. (Remember that outside the EU most trading countries speak English and use our imperial measures and weights system.)

By forcing us to follow their daft rules the EU is successfully wrecking our competitiveness.

The EU wants our money (we are net contributors to the EU). They want our oil, our gold and our well stocked pension funds. And they want a clear entry to our markets for their goods.

The bottom line is that England would be richer and much more successful outside the EU.

264

Accused prisoners in English courts will soon not have the right to see evidence against them before they are committed for trial. That's in response to an EU ruling.

265

Another EU ruling means that the prosecution will soon be able to continue trying a defendant until they get a 'guilty' verdict. Double jeopardy is coming to a courtroom near you.

266

Other countries within the EU get huge handouts at England's expense. For example, both the Germans and the Spanish produce subsidised coal which is twice as expensive as ours would be if we hadn't closed our unprofitable mines.

267

It seems impossible that the EU will allow one nation to exist with more than a dozen different languages. I have no doubt whatsoever that there are plans ahead to make English the standard European language. There will be rioting in the streets when the French find out, but it will by then be far too late.

Indeed, there is evidence showing that this has already started. For example, medical records and reports in France must already be written in English and school children throughout Europe are now being taught English to a high standard.

I suspect that it will not be many years before the official business of the EU will be conducted almost, if not entirely, exclusively in English. With English the language of choice in America how long will it be before world leaders are quietly pointing out the huge advantages of a world government?

This is undoubtedly one of many reasons why the EU's leaders are desperate for England to join the euro.

In emergencies, when there are no translators present, EU officials and members are already told to speak in English – which has now become euroland's base language.

268

Customs duties collected at all English ports go directly to the EU. In addition, the EU takes 1 per cent of all our VAT revenue and a third of one percent of our total GDP. When England, as a nation, does well we have to pay more to the EU and so the Government has to put up taxes. In 1998, for example, England had to pay an extra £530 million to the EU (on top of our usual massive payment) because we had had a good year. In that same year, Germany got a bonus rebate of £840 million and France received a bonus payment of £600 million from the EU. Poor old Italy had to make do with a cash hand-out bonus of £474 million. England never receives money from the EU.

269

'Even those who once preached decentralisation, always abandon their doctrine
on coming to power. You can be sure of that.'
ALEXIS DE TOCQUEVILLE

270

The EU is composed of countries which are largely Catholic and there seems little doubt that as the years go by, the English Protestant church will be marginalised more and more.

When England asked if we could put the Queen's head on our euro coins (if we joined), the answer was a definite 'no' on the grounds that the Queen isn't Catholic while much of Europe is. It was thought that having the Queen's head on euros would be offensive to Catholics.

However, the Vatican City mints euro coins with the Pope's head on one side. No one in the EU seems to consider that that might cause offence to Protestants, Muslims or Jews. No one in the EU seemed to think that the fact that the Pope has refused to condemn IRA terrorists might offend some English folk.

271

There are plans in England to lift the ban on Catholics sitting on the English throne.

272

If Catholics are asked 'Who, sir, do you hold for? The Queen of England or the Bishop of Rome?' they have to say the Bishop of Rome or be excommunicated.

273

The Single European Act and Final Act 1985 was pushed through Parliament as a sub-clause in a minor Foreign Office bill which was debated by a handful of MPs. The crucial clause, handing England over to the EU, was not debated. When the Bill got to the House of Lords, the Government accidentally issued two order papers. An order paper carrying the correct date went to peers who would vote for the Bill. An order paper with the incorrect date went to the rest. Not surprisingly, the bill was passed. And thus was England betrayed. The Single European Act and Final Act 1985 allows for qualified majority voting in the EU. It is this Act which allows the EU to decide what happens to England. A protest vote from England will be of no value.

274

England's EU Commissioners must swear an oath of loyalty to the EU. The EU claims superiority over the Queen of England. The EU claims that its laws take precedence over English laws.

275

No official translation of the Amsterdam Treaty has ever been published. But the Treaty allows the EU to impose its will on member states whether they agree or not. The EU can force England to accept the euro.

276

It will soon be possible for the EU to ban English people from flying the Union Jack or the cross of St. George on the grounds that to do so would be racist and possibly offensive to individuals of other nationalities living in England.

277

It will soon be possible for the EU to ban books (such as this one) which criticise the EU.

278

Knowing that they probably won't win a referendum to replace the pound with the euro, sneaky Government ministers are planning to bring the euro into England through the back door. In the summer of 2002 businesses in one part of Wales were instructed to accept the euro alongside the pound as a valid currency. Many locals were opposed to the plan which was imposed with EU and Government support.

279

Over £5 billion is lost in the EU each year because of corruption. The money just disappears. No one does anything about this.

280

How much of this did you know?

281

Under EU law it will be possible for the Europol officers to arrest English citizens on suspicion of *intending* to commit a crime. The 'thought police' are here.

282

So why does the EU exist at all? Who benefits?

283

In 1937, Adolf Hitler (who had, incidentally, been the first to use the phrase United States of Europe) developed the idea of getting rid of European nations and establishing regions instead. He wanted to create a united Europe and to destroy national identities. He wanted to get rid of national boundaries and create new regions to be ruled from Berlin.

In June 1940, Hermann Goerring made the first reference to the European Economic Community. In 1942, Heydricht published *The Reich Plan for the Domination of Europe* – a document which bears the odd similarity to the Treaty of Rome. In March 1943, 13 countries (including France and Italy) were invited to join a new European federation which would be under German military control. In August 1944, the heads of the Nazi Government and a group of leading German industrialists met at a hotel in Strasbourg and decided to hide fairly large amounts of money so that the fight for a German dominated united Europe could continue after the end of the war. They were worried that this was the only way Germany could dominate the peace if it lost the war. They realised that their back-up plan would take years to reach fruition.

284

You should be afraid of the EU. But you can do much to save yourself, your friends, your family and your future.

285

A Dozen Great English Politicians Who Would Have
Fought Against The Euro And The EU

Winston Churchill
Benjamin Disraeli
William Pitt (the younger)
William Pitt (the elder)
Robert Walpole
Robert Peel
Ernest Bevin
Viscount Palmerston
Oliver Cromwell
Clement Attlee
Herbert Asquith
Stanley Baldwin

286

Here's another thought.

It was when Germany unilaterally recognised Bosnia that the break up of Yugoslavia began. The Germans then recognised Slovenia and Croatia. Germany has gained enormously from all this and now has great influence throughout Eastern Europe.

Curiously, the EU is expanding eastwards with Eastern European countries (many of which are little more than German provinces) being brought into the EU fold.

287

'Truth is on the march and nothing will stop it.'
EMILE ZOLA

288

Could England survive outside the EU? Yes. Very well, thank you.

There has for years now been a cynical and ruthless propaganda campaign to persuade us that England has no future outside Europe. This is nonsense. For example, take Switzerland. They ignored the encouragement of their Government and voted against joining the EU. But they have negotiated for themselves an excellent trade agreement – thereby putting a lie to the utterly false claim that no European country can possibly survive unless it becomes part of the EU.

The europhiles constantly argue that England would be ruined if she left Europe.

Oh, what porkies these people do tell.

As *The Economist* said recently: '...the idea that leaving (the EU) would be 'economic suicide' is nonsense'.

Examine what would happen if England pulled up the Tunnel and stopped paying subs to the big EU in Brussels:

1. The EU would impose its external tariff on English exports to Europe. This would make very little difference to English companies – most of whose exports go outside Europe anyway. The World Trade Organisation restricts the EU to an external tariff of around six per cent so the effect would, in any case, be quite small. (England would almost certainly be able to negotiate for itself a smaller tariff – in the way that Switzerland has. This would drive down the cost of leaving the EU still further.)

2. If outside the EU, England would, inevitably, be outside the euro. There would be an exchange rate between the pound and the euro. In the long run this could well be to England's advantage.

3. The external tariff on England's imports from outside the EU would disappear. England would probably gain more from this

than it would lose from the imposition of a tariff on English exports to Europe.

4. An England outside the EU would be able to make special trading deals with other countries – such as those in the Commonwealth. This could be hugely advantageous.

5. Europhiles claim that if England left the EU then countries from outside Europe (such as Japan and America) would invest less. This is nonsense. England attracts more outside investment (known to economists as 'Foreign Direct Investment') than other European countries because its labour market is still relatively unregulated. If it was outside the EU, England could take advantage of its independence to reduce the number of regulations limiting foreign companies. EU regulations are already regarded as a minefield. Just ask some of the foreign companies who have had eurocrats leaping up and down all over them. Many would jump at the chance to invest in a less regulated part of Europe.

Finally, even if FDI did fall, England would not necessarily lose, since in an often irrational attempt to encourage foreign businesses (at the expense of English businesses) the English Government subsidises these investments. A subsidised outside investment may well not make money for the country!

The bottom line is that the English stand to lose nothing by leaving the EU.

If England left the EU it would leave behind an incompetent and power-hungry bureaucracy which has consistently failed. If we left the EU they would not be able to do anything in revenge. Remember, we have a trade deficit with the EU. (For example, we have a trade deficit of over £3 billion a year with Germany alone.) The EU countries desperately need our trade.

English politicians have supported the EU, lied and deceived the English voters and signed away rights and freedoms. They often did this claiming that they wanted England to have influence in Europe.

This is nonsense.

England has far less influence in Europe than it had ten, twenty or thirty years ago.

Politicians have sold out the voters to gain personal political influence.

England, and the English, have gained nothing from membership of the EU. But membership has cost a great deal.

England would survive and survive well outside the EU.

The people of Norway and Switzerland have voted against joining the EU – and have thrived. Greenland, once in the EU, escaped and has prospered since getting out. If they can do it so can England.

England would survive well outside the EU. It would be richer and more powerful. And its citizens would regain their lost independence.

England's trade is in surplus with every state in the world except the EU. If England left the EU it could regain power over its own legal system, armed forces, and agricultural policies. Hundreds of thousands of small businesses would be saved from suffocating bureaucracy.

English is the world's leading business language. English dominates the internet. Our language means that we can trade with any other country in the world.

Tony Blair won't tell you this but England would be much richer if it left the EU. We would save a fortune. And be free of 30,000 rules.

The only people who would lose would be the politicians for whom the English stage is too small.

We can still leave the EU.

289

'When the government fears the people, there is liberty. When the people fear the government, there is tyranny.'
THOMAS JEFFERSON

290

The EU now has 11 official languages. By the year 2004 it will have 21 official languages. When the number of official languages grows to 21, the possible interpreting combinations will leap to 420 (from 110 today). The EU will have to find (and pay) tens of thousands of skilled, reliable, honest interpreters who are prepared to move to Brussels and who can translate Estonian into Polish, Czech into Maltese or Estonian into Hungarian. The potential for error or misinterpretation grows with every translation. The EU already employs 3,500 full time interpreters. Every rule, every regulation, every directive, every comment has (in theory, at least) to be translated into every one of those 11 official languages. Every remark in the EU parliament has to be translated into 10 other languages. A huge portion of the EU budget goes into translating all these documents. Romano Prodi, President of the European Commission has stated that: 'the ability for EU citizens to interact with the European institutions in a language of their own country is a fundamental prerequisite of a democratic Europe'.

291

It will soon be illegal to withdraw from the EU. Even talking or writing (or possibly thinking) about leaving will be illegal.

292

Remember constantly that it was Hitler's intention to unite Europe. (Just as it had been the ambitions of Charlemagne, Charles V, Louis XIV, Napoleon and the Kaiser.) Remember that it was Adolf Hitler who first used the phrase 'The United States of Europe'. Remember that it was Hitler who had the idea of establishing regions of Europe in order to destroy national identities. He wanted to break European nations into regions so that they could be ruled from Berlin.

Does that simple and ignoble ambition remind you of anything? It ought to. That is exactly what EU policy is now – although for various historical reasons Berlin has been replaced by the more neutral Brussels.

And can you remember where the term European Economic Community comes from?

The increasingly rabid proponents of the EU won't tell you this, and may be embarrassed at my having had the ill grace to drag it up, but it was Hermann Goerring who made the first reference to the European Economic Community. Goerring is the true father of the EEC, though the europhiles tend to forget to give him the credit.

Remember that Hitler and Mussolini (the original fascists) wanted to unite Europe. They were true Europeans. They would be thrilled to bits to see the new EU in action.

Europhiles may not like to be reminded of it (and reminding them of it is quite possibly against the law) but Blair and the other pro-fascist pro-Europeans are committed to furthering Goerring's vision.

Wave your country's flag with pride. Be proud to be English (French, German, Scottish, Welsh or whatever). We are none of us Europeans.

Europe is not a country. Neither the EU nor the euro will survive.

We do have a choice: subservience or a quiet, non violent revolution.

293

In 1962, Field Marshal Montgomery found Sir Winston Churchill sitting up in bed smoking a cigar. Churchill shouted for more brandy and protested against Britain's proposed entry into the Common Market.

294

If you want to help save England and your freedom buy copies of this book (available from Publishing House) and distribute them to your friends, relatives and neighbours. Together we can change the way the future would have been.

295

'The game's afoot:
Follow your spirit; and upon this charge
Cry 'God for Harry! England and Saint George!'
WILLIAM SHAKESPEARE

For a catalogue of Vernon Coleman's books please write to:

Publishing House
Trinity Place
Barnstaple
Devon EX32 9HJ
England

Telephone	01271 328892
Fax	01271 328768

Outside the UK:

Telephone	+44 1271 328892
Fax	+44 1271 328768

Or visit our website:

www.vernoncoleman.com